A Concert of Tenses

Poets on Poetry   Donald Hall, General Editor

Tess Gallagher

A Concert
of Tenses

ESSAYS ON POETRY

Ann Arbor
The University of Michigan Press

1990   1989   5   4   3

Library of Congress Cataloging-in-Publication Data

Gallagher, Tess.
    A concert of tenses.

    (Poets on poetry)
    Includes bibliographies.
    1. Gallagher, Tess—Authorship. 2. Gallagher, Tess—
Interviews. 3. Poets, American—20th century—
Interviews. 4. Poetry. I. Title. II. Series.
PS3557.A41156Z464 1986   811'.5'09   86-19287
ISBN 0-472-09370-3 (alk. paper)
ISBN 0-472-06370-7 (pbk. : alk. paper)

For Raymond Carver

Acknowledgments

Grateful acknowledgment is made to the following individuals, journals, and publishers for permission to reprint previously published materials.

American Poetry Review for "Adding to the Unhappiness: Those Poems You Are Writing," *American Poetry Review* 8, no. 5 (1979); for "Last Class with Roethke," originally published as "A Poet at the MLA," *American Poetry Review* 9, no. 2 (1980); for "My Father's Love Letters," *American Poetry Review* 10, no. 3 (1981); for "Inside the Kaleidoscope: The Poetry of Michael Burkard," *American Poetry Review* 11, no. 3 (1982); and for "The Poem as a Reservoir for Grief," *American Poetry Review* 13, no. 4 (1984).

The Atlantic for "The Poem as Time Machine," *The Atlantic*, May, 1980. Copyright Tess Gallagher.

Stephen Berg for "Sing It Rough" from *Singular Voices,* edited by Stephen Berg (New York: Avon Books, 1985). Copyright © 1985.

Rachel Berghash and WBAI-FM for "An Interview with Tess Gallagher," broadcast on WBAI-FM, New York, May, 1985.

Graywolf Press for "Black Money," "Stepping Outside," and "Two Stories" from *Instructions to the Double,* copyright © 1976 by Tess Gallagher; for "My Mother Remembers That She Was Beautiful" from *Under Stars,* copyright © 1978 by Tess Gallagher; and for "Sudden Journey," "3 A.M. Kitchen: My Father Talking," "Each Bird Walking," "Linoleum," and "In That Time When It Was Not the Fashion" from *Willingly,* copyright © 1984 by Tess Gallagher.

Ironwood for "A Concert of Tenses," *Ironwood* 14 (Fall 1979); for "Like a Strange Guest of the Earth: The Poems of Linda Gregg," *Ironwood* 15 (Spring 1980); and for "Again: Some Thoughts on the

Narrative Impulse in Contemporary Poetry," *Ironwood* 24 (Fall 1984).

Parnassus: Poetry in Review for "Scarves! Echoes! Pavilions!," *Parnassus* 6, no. 1 (Fall/Winter 1977); for "Poetry in Translation: Literary Imperialism, or Defending the Musk Ox," *Parnassus* 9, no. 1 (Spring/Summer 1981); and for "Throwing the Scarecrows from the Garden," *Parnassus* 12, no. 2 (Spring/Summer 1985); 13, no. 1 (Fall/Winter 1985).

Sheep Meadow Press for "To Work and Keep Kind" from *A Celebration for Stanley Kunitz: On His Eightieth Birthday.* Copyright © 1986.

Every effort has been made to trace the ownership of all copyrighted material in this book and to obtain permission for its use.

Contents

My father, Leslie Bond, holding me on his mother's porch in Port Angeles, Washington, in 1944

My Father's Love Letters

It's two days before Christmas and I have checked myself into the Dewitt Ranch Motel. "We don't ask questions here," says the manager, handing me the key to number 66. I let him think what he thinks.

The room is what I need, what I've been imagining for the past two days—a place with much passing and no record. I feel guilty about spending the money, but I've trusted my instincts about what it will take to get this writing done. For the past week I've been absorbed with student manuscripts and term papers. At the finish, I discover I have all but vanished. Coming to the motel is a way to trick myself out of anonymity, to urge my identity to rise like cream to the top again.

I had known from the first moments of being asked to write about my influences as a writer that I would want to get back to the child in me. For to talk of influences for a writer is essentially to trace the development of a psychic and spiritual history, to go back to where it keeps starting as you think about it, as an invention of who you are becoming. The history which has left its deepest imprint on me has been an oral and actual history and so involves my willingness at a very personal level. It involves people no one will ever know again. People like the motel room I write this in, full of passing and no record. The "no record" part is where I come in. I must try to interrupt their silence. Articulate it and so resurrect them so that homage can be paid.

To speak of influences, then, is not to say "Here, try this," only "This happened and this is what I think of it at this moment of writing."

I want to begin with rain. A closeness, a need for rain. It is the climate of my psyche and I would not fully have known this if I had not spent a year in Arizona, where it rained only three glorious times during my entire stay there. I begin with rain also because it is a way of introducing my birthplace on the Olympic peninsula in Washington State, the town of Port Angeles. The rain forest is a few miles west. The rain is more violent and insistent there. Port Angeles lies along the strait of Juan de Fuca and behind the town are the Olympic Mountains. The Japanese current brings in warm air, striking the mountains, which are snow-covered into June.

It is a faithful rain. You feel it has some allegiance to the trees and the people, to the little harbor with its long arm of land which makes a band of calm for the fishing boats and for the rafts of logs soon to be herded to the mills. Inside or outside the wood-framed houses, the rain pervades the temperament of the people. It brings an ongoing thoughtfulness to their faces, a meditativeness that causes them to fall silent for long periods, to stand at their windows looking out at nothing in particular. The people don't mind getting wet. Galoshes, umbrellas—there isn't a market for them here. The people walk in the rain as within some spirit they wish not to offend with resistance. Most of them have not been to Arizona. They know the rain is a reason for not living where they live, but they live there anyway. They work hard in the logging camps, in the pulp mills and lumberyards. Everything has a wetness over it, glistening quietly as though it were still in the womb, waiting to be born.

Sudden Journey

Maybe I'm seven in the open field—
the straw-grass so high
only the top of my head makes a curve
of brown in the yellow. Rain then.
First a little. A few drops on my
wrist, the right wrist. More rain.
My shoulders, my chin. Until I'm looking up
to let my eyes take the bliss.

I open my face. Let the teeth show. I
pull my shirt down past the collar-bones.
I'm still a boy under my breast spots.
I can drink anywhere. The rain. My
skin shattering. Up suddenly, needing
to gulp, turning with my tongue, my arms out
running, running in the hard, cold plenitude
of all those who reach earth by falling.

Growing up there, I thought the moss-light that lived with us lived everywhere. It was a sleepy predawn light that muted the landscape and made the trees come close. I always went outside with my eyes wide, no need to shield them from sun bursts or the steady assault of skies I was to know later in El Paso or Tucson. The colors of green and gray are what bind me to the will to write poems.

Along with rain and a subdued quality of light, I have needed the nearness of water. I said once in an interview that if Napoleon had stolen his battle plans from the dreams of his sleeping men, then maybe I had stolen my poems from the gray presence of water.

The house I grew up in overlooks the eighteen-mile stretch of water between Canada and America at its far northwest reach. The freighters, tankers, tugs, and small fishing boats pass daily; and even at night a water star, the light on a mast, might mark a vessel's passage through the strait. My father was a longshoreman for many of these years and he knew the names of the ships and what they were carrying and where they came from: the *Kenyo Maru* (Japanese), the *Eastern Grace* (Liberian), the *Bright Hope* (Taiwanese), the *Brilliant Star* (Panamanian), the *Shoshei Maru* (Japanese)—pulp for paper, logs for plywood, lumber for California. He explained that *maru* was a word that meant that the ship would make its return home. I have been like these ships, always pointed on a course of return to this town and its waters.

On Saturdays my father would drive my mother and my three brothers and me into town to shop and then to wait for him while he drank in what we called the "beer joints." We would sit for hours in the car, watching the townspeople pass. I noticed what they carried, how they walked, their gestures as they looked into the store windows. In other cars were women and families waiting as we were, for men in taverns. In the life of a child, these periods of stillness in parked cars were small eternities. The only release or amusement was to see things, and to wonder about them. Since the making of images is for me perhaps 90 percent seeing and 10 percent word power, this car seeing and the stillness it enforced contributed to a patience and a curiosity that heightened my ability to see. The things to be seen from a parked car were not spectacular, but they were what we had—and they promoted a fascination with the ordinary. My mother was an expert at this: "See that little girl with the pigtails. I bet she's never had her hair cut. Look there, her father's taking her in there where the men get their hair cut." And sure enough, the little girl would emerge twenty minutes later, eyes red from crying, one hand in her father's and the other clutching a small paper sack. "The pigtails are in there."

Every hour or so my mother would send me on a round of the taverns to try for a sighting of my father. I would peck on the windows and the barmaid would shake her head *no* or motion down the dim aisle of faces to where my father would be sitting on his stool, forgetting, forgetting us all for a while.

My father's drinking, and the quarrels he had with my mother because of it, terrorized my childhood. There is no other way to put it. And if coping with terror and anxiety are necessary to the psychic stamina of a poet, I had them in steady doses—just as inevitably as I had the rain. I learned that the world was not just, that any balance was temporary, that unreasonableness could descend at any minute, thrashing aside everything and everyone in its path.

Emotional and physical vulnerability was a constant. Yet the heart began to take shelter, to build understandings out of words. It seems that a poet is one who must be strong enough to live in the unprotected openness, yet not so strong that the heart enters what the Russian poet Akhmatova calls "the icy calm of unloving." Passion and forgiveness, emotional fortitude—these were the lessons of the heart I had no choice but to learn in my childhood. I wonder now what kept me from the calm of not loving. Perhaps it was the unspoken knowledge that love, my parents' love, through all was constant, though its blows could rake the quick of my being.

I was sixteen when I had my last lesson from the belt and my father's arm. I stood still in the yard, in full view of the neighbors. I looked steadily ahead, without tears or cries, as a tree must look while the saw bites in, then deepens to the core. I felt my spirit reach its full defiance. I stood somehow in the power of my womanhood that day and knew I had passed beyond humiliation. I felt my father's arm begin to know I had outleaped the pain. It came down harder. If pain could not find me, what then would enforce control and fear?

I say I entered my womanhood because I connect womanhood with a strong, enduring aspect of my being. I am aware, looking back, that women even more than children often serve a long apprenticeship to physically and psychically inflicted threat and pain. Perhaps because of this they learn more readily what the slave, the hostage, the prisoner, also know—the ultimate freedom of the spirit. They learn how unreasonable treatment and physical pain may be turned aside by an act of will. This freedom of spirit is what has enabled poets down through the ages to record the courage and hopes of entire peoples even in times of oppression. That women have not had a larger share in the history of such poetry has always seemed a mystery to me, considering the wealth of spiritual power that suffering often brings when it does not kill or maim the spirit. I can only assume that words have been slow in coming to women because their days have, until recently, been given over so wholly to acts, to doing and caring for.

During these periods of abuse I did not stop loving. It was our hurt not to have another way to settle these things. For my father and I had no language between us in those numb years of my changing. All through my attempts in the poems, I have needed to forge a language that would give these dead and living lives a way to speak. There was often the feeling that the language might come too late, might even do damage, might not be equal to the love. All these fears. Finally no choice.

The images of these two primal figures, mother and father, condense now into a vision of my father's work-thickened hands, and my mother's back, turned in hopeless anger at the stove where she fixed eggs for my father in silence. My father gets up from the table, shows me the open palms of his hands. "Threasie," he says, "get an education. Don't get hands like these."

Out of this moment and others like it I think I began to make a formula which translates roughly: words = more than physical power = freedom from enslavement to job-life = power to direct and make meaning in your own life.

There were few examples of my parents' having used words to transcend the daily. The only example was perhaps my father's love letters. They were kept in a cedar chest at the foot of my bed. One day I came across them, under a heap of hand-embroidered pillowcases. There were other treasures there, like the deer horn used to call the hounds when my father had hunted as a young man. The letters were written on lined tablet paper with a yellow cast to it. Written with a pencil in a consistently erratic hand, signed "Les" for Leslie and punctuated with a brigade of XXXXXs. I would stare at these Xs, as though they contained some impenetrable clue as to why this man and woman had come together. The letters were mainly informational—he had worked here, was going there, had seen so-and-so, would be coming back to Missouri at such and such a time. But also there was humor, harmless jokes some workman had told him, and little teasings that only my mother could have interpreted.

My mother's side of the correspondence was missing, probably because my father had thrown her letters away or lost them during the Depression years when he crossed the country, riding the rails, working in the cotton fields, the oil fields, and the coal mines. My mother's lost letters are as important to remember as those I found from my father. They were the now invisible lifeline that answered and provoked my father's heart-scrawl across the miles and days of their long courtship.

My father on his fishing boat in Port Angeles, Washington, in 1970. *Photograph by Lawrence Gallagher.*

I might easily have called this essay "My Mother's Love Letters," for they would have represented the most articulate half of the correspondence, had they been saved. That they are now irrevocably lost, except to the imagination, moves them into the realm of speculation. The very fact that my mother had saved my father's love letters became a sign to me as a child that love *had* existed between my parents, no matter what acts and denials had come after.

As with my parents, invisible love has been an undercurrent in my poems, in the tone of them, perhaps. They have, when I can manage it, what Marianne Moore called iodine and what I call turpentine. A rawness of impulse, a sharpness, a tension, that complicates the emotion, that withholds even as it gives. This is a proclivity of being, the signature of a nature that had learned perhaps wrongheadedly that love too openly seen becomes somehow inauthentic, unrealized.

My father's love letters were then the only surviving record of my parents' courtship and, indeed, the only record that they ever loved each other, for they never showed affection for one another in front of us. On a fishing trip years after I'd left home, my father was to remark that they had written to each other for over ten years before they married in 1941.

My father's sleep was like the rain. It permeated the household. When he was home he seemed always to be sleeping. We saw him come home and we saw him leave. We saw him during the evening meal. The talk then was of the ILWU longshoremen's union and of the men he worked with. He worked hard. It could be said that he never missed a day's work. It was a fact I used in his defense when I thought my mother was too hard on him after a drinking bout.

Stanley Kunitz has seen the archetypal search for the father as a frequent driving force for some poets, his own father having committed suicide before his birth. It occurs to me that in my own case, the father was among the living dead, and this made my situation all the more urgent. It was as if I had set myself the task of waking him before it was too late. I seemed to need to tell him who he was and that what was happening to him mattered and was witnessed by at least one other. This is why he has been so much at the center of my best efforts in the poems.

The first poem I wrote that reached him was called "Black Money," this image taken from the way shoveling sulfur at the pulp mills had turned his money black. He had come to visit me in the Seattle apartment where I lived as a student and I remember telling him I'd written this poem for his birthday. I had typed it and sealed it into an envelope like a secret message. He seemed embarrassed, as if about to be left out of something. Then he tore the envelope open and unfolded the poem. He handed it back to me. "You read it to me," he said. I read the poem to him and as I read I could feel the need in his listening. I had finally reached him. "Now that's something," he said when I'd finished. "I'm going to show that to the boys down on the dock."

Black Money

His lungs heaving all day in a sulphur mist,
then dusk, the lunch pail torn from him
before he reaches the house, his children
a cloud of swallows about him.
At the stove in the tumbled rooms, the wife,
her back the wall he fights most, and she
with no weapon but silence
and to keep him from the bed.

In their sleep the mill hums and turns
at the edge of water. Blue smoke
swells the night and they drift
from the graves they have made for each other,
float out from the open-mouthed sleep
of their children, past banks and businesses,
the used car lots, liquor store, the swings in the park.

The mill burns on, now a burst of cinders,
now whistles screaming down the bay, saws jagged
in half light. Then like a whip
the sun across the bed, windows high with mountains
and the sleepers fallen to pillows
as gulls fall, tilting

against their shadows on the log booms.
Again the trucks shudder the wood framed houses
passing to the mill. My father
snorts, splashes in the bathroom,
throws open our doors to cowboy music
on the radio, hearts are cheating,
somebody is alone, there's blood in Tulsa.
Out the back yard the night-shift men rattle
the gravel in the alley going home.
My father fits goggles to his head.

From his pocket he takes anything metal,
the pearl-handled jack knife, a ring of keys,
and for us, black money shoveled
from the sulphur pyramids heaped in the distance
like yellow gold. Coffee bottle tucked in his armpit
he swaggers past the chicken coop,
a pack of cards at his breast.
In a fan of light beyond him
the Kino Maru pulls out for Seattle,
some black star climbing
the deep globe of his eye.

As the oldest child, I seemed to serve my parents' lives
in an ambassadorial capacity. But I was an ambassador with-
out a country, for the household was perpetually on the verge
of dissolving. I cannot say how many times I watched my
father go down the walk to the picket fence, leaving us for-
ever, pausing long enough at the gate to look back at us
huddled on the porch. "Who's coming with me?" he would
ask. No one moved. Again and again we abandoned each
other.

Maybe this was the making of my refugee mentality. And
perhaps when you are an emotional refugee you learn to be
industrious toward the prospect of love and shelter. You
know both are fragile and that stability must lie with you or it
is nowhere. You make a home of yourself. Words for me and
later poems were the tools of that home-making.

Even when you think you are only a child and have nothing,
there are things you have, and as Sartre has already told us,
one of these things is words. When I saw I had words and that

these could affect what happened to me and those I loved, I felt less powerless, as though these might win through, might at least mediate in a life ruled as much by chance as by intention.

These ambassadorial skills I was learning as a child were an odd kind of training for the writing of poems, perhaps, but they were just that. For in the writing of the poem you must represent both sides of the question. If not in fact, then in understanding. You must bring them into dialogue with one another fairly, without the bias of causes or indignation or needing too much to be right. It requires a widening of perspective, away from oversimplification—the strict good or bad, wrong or rightness of a situation. The sensibility I've been attempting to write out of wants to represent the spectrum of awareness. In this way the life is accounted for in its fullness, when I am able.

I have spoken of words as a stay against unreasonableness, and they are often this—though more to one's solitude than to the actual life. My father came to his own words late, but in time. I was to discover that at seventy he could entertain my poet friends and would be spoken of afterward as someone exceptional in their experience. He told stories, was witty, liked to laugh. But in those early days, my father was not a man you could talk with. He would drive me to my piano lessons, the family's one luxury, without speaking. He smoked cigarettes, one after the other. He was thinking and driving. If he had had anything to drink during these times it was best to give him a wide berth. I was often afraid of him, of the violence in him, though like the rain, tenderness was there, unspoken and with a fiber that strangely informed even the unreasonable. If to be a poet is to balance contraries, to see how seemingly opposite qualities partake of, in fact penetrate, each other, I learned this from my combative parents.

3 A.M. Kitchen: My Father Talking

For years it was land working me, oil fields,
cotton fields, then I got some land. I

worked it. Them days you could just about
make a living. I was logging.

Then I sent to Missouri. Momma
come out. We got married.
We got some kids. Five kids.
That kept us going.

We bought some land near the water.
It was cheap then. The water
was right there. You just looked out
the window. It never left the window.

I bought a boat. Fourteen footer.
There was fish out there then.
You remember, we used to catch
six, eight fish, clean them right
out in the yard. I could of fished to China.

I quit the woods. One day just
walked out, took off my corks, said that's
it. I went to the docks.
I was driving winch. You had to watch
to see nothing fell out of the sling. If
you killed somebody you'd
never forget it. All
those years I was just working
I was on edge, every day. Just working.

You kids. I could tell you
a lot. But I won't.

It's winter. I play a lot of cards
down at the tavern. Your mother.
I have to think of excuses
to get out of the house. You're
wasting your time, she says. You're wasting
your money.

You don't have no idea, Threasie.
I run out of things
to work for. Hell, why shouldn't I
play cards? Threasie,
some days now I just don't know.

This long childhood period of living without surety con-
tributed in another way to my urge to write poetry. If I had to

give one word which serves my poetry more than any other, it might be "uncertainty." Uncertainty which leads to exploration, to the articulation of fears, to the loss of the kind of confidence that provides answers too quickly, too superficially. It is the poet's uncertainty which leaves her continually in an openness to the possibilities of being and saying. The true materials of poetry are essentially invisible—a capacity for the constant emptying of the house of the word, turning it out homeless and humbled to search its way toward meaning again. Maybe "poem" for me is the act of a prolonged beginning, one without resolution except perhaps musically, rhythmically—the word "again" engraved on the fiery hammer.

After my youngest brother's death when I was twenty, I began to recognize the ability of poetry to extend the lives of those not present except as memory. My brother's death was the official beginning of my mortality. It filled my life, all our lives, with the sense of an unspoken bond, a pain which traveled with us in memory. It was as though memory were a kind of flickering shadow left behind by those who died. This caused me to connect memory firmly to the life of the spirit and finally to write poems which formalized the sharing of that memory.

I have been writing about my progress toward a life in words and poems, but my first love was actually paint. As a child I took great pleasure in the smell of linseed, the oil of it on my fingers, the tubes of oil paint with their bands of approximate color near the caps, the long-handled brushes. I had heard somewhere that artists taught themselves by copying other painters. But the only paintings we had in the house were those in some Bible books a salesman had sold my mother. I began to copy these with oil colors onto some rough paper I'd found in a boxcar near the paper mill below our house. I remember especially my painting of Jacob sleeping at the foot of a heavenly stairway, with several angels descending. They each had a pair of huge wings, and I wondered at the time why they didn't just fly down, instead of using the stairs. The faces of these angels occupied a great deal of my efforts. And I think it is some help to being a poet to paint the faces of angels when you are ten.

I finished the Jacob painting and sent it to my grandfather in Missouri. He was a farmer and owned a thousand-acre farm of scrub oak, farmland, and riverbed in the Ozarks. My mother had been raised there. Often when she had a faraway look about her, I imagined she was visiting there in her thoughts.

My Mother Remembers That She Was Beautiful

The falling snow has made her thoughtful
and young in the privacy
of our table with its netted candle
and thick white plates. The serious faces
of the lights breathe on the pine boards
behind her. She is visiting
the daughter never close
or far enough away to come to.

She keeps her coat on, called into
her girlhood by such forgetting
I am gone or yet
to happen. She sees herself
among the townspeople, the country glances
slow with fields and sky
as she passes or waits
with a brother in the hot animal smell
of the auction stand: sunlight,
straw hats, a dog's tail
brushing her bare leg.

"There are things you know.
I didn't have to beg," she said, "for anything."

The beautiful one speaks to me
from the changed, proud face and I see
how little I've let her know
of what she becomes. Years
were never the trouble, or the white hair
I braided near the sea
on a summer day. Who
she must have been
is lost to me through some fault
in my own reflection and we will have to go on
as we think we are, walking for no one's sake

from the empty restaurant into the one color
of the snow—before us, the close houses,
the brave and wondering lights of the houses.

Children sometimes adopt a second father or mother when they are cut off from the natural parent. Porter Morris, my uncle, was the father I could speak with. He lived with my grandparents on the farm in Windyville, Missouri, where I spent many of my childhood summers. He never married, but stayed with the farm even after my grandparents died. He'd been a mule trainer during the Second World War, the only time he had ever left home. He loved horses and raised and gentled one for me, which he named Angel Foot because she was black except for one white foot.

I continued to visit my grandfather and my uncle during the five years of my first marriage. My husband was a jet pilot in the Marine Corps. We were stationed in the South, so I would go to cook for my uncle during the haying and I would also help stack the hay in the barn. My uncle and I took salt to the cattle. We sowed a field with barley and went to market in Springfield with a truckload of pigs. There were visits with neighbors, Cleydeth and Joe Stefter or Jule Elliot, when we sat for hours telling stories and gossiping. Many images from my uncle's stories and from these visits to the farm got into the long poem "Songs of the Runaway Bride" in my first book.

My uncle lived alone at the farm after my grandfather's death, but soon he met a woman who lived with her elderly parents. He began to remodel an old house on the farm. There was talk of marriage. One day my mother called to say there had been a fire at the farm. The house had burned to the ground and my uncle could not be found. She returned to the farm, what remained of her childhood home. After the ashes had cooled, she searched with the sheriff and found my uncle's skeleton where it had burned into the mattress springs of the bed.

My mother would not accept the coroner's verdict that the fire had been caused by an electrical short-circuit, or a fire in the chimney. It was summer and no fire would have been laid.

She combed the ashes looking for the shotgun my uncle always kept near his bed and the other gun, a rifle, he hunted with. They were not to be found. My mother believed her brother had been murdered and she set about proving it. She offered a reward and soon after, a young boy walking along the roadside picked my uncle's billfold out of the ditch, his name stamped in gold on the flap.

Three men were eventually brought to trial. I journeyed to Bolivar, Missouri, to meet my parents for the trial. We watched as the accused killer was released and the other two men, who had confessed to being his accomplices, were sentenced to five years in the penitentiary for manslaughter. Parole would be possible for them in two to three years. The motive had been money, although one of the men had held a grudge against my uncle for having been ordered to move out of a house he'd been renting from my uncle some three years before. They had taken forty dollars from my uncle, then shot him when he could not give them more. My parents and I came away from the trial stunned with disbelief and anger.

Two Stories

to the author of a story taken from the death of my uncle, Porter Morris, killed June 7, 1972

You kept the names, the flies
of who they were, mine
gone carnival, ugly Tessie.
It got wilder but nothing
personal. The plot had me
an easy lay for a buck.
My uncle came to life
as my lover. At 16
the murderer stabbed cows
and mutilated chickens. Grown,
you gave him a crowbar that happened
to be handy twice. Then you made him
do it alone. For me
it took three drunks, a gun, the house

on fire. There was a black space
between trees where I told you.

The shape of my uncle
spread its arms on the wire springs
in the yard and the neighbors
came to look at his shadow
caught there under the nose
of his dog. They left that angel
to you. Your killer never
mentioned money. Like us he wanted
to outlive his hand in the sure blood
of another. The veins of my uncle streaked
where the house had been. They watched
until morning. Your man found a faucet
in an old man's side. His pants
were stiff with it for days. He left
the crowbar on Tessie's porch like a bone.

My weapon was never found.
The murderers drove a white
stationwagon and puked
as they went. They hoped
for 100 dollar bills stuffed
in a lard can. But a farmer
keeps his money in cattle
and land. They threw his billfold
into the ditch like an empty
bird. One ran away. Two stayed
with women. I kept the news
blind. You took it from my mouth,
shaped it for the market, still
a dream worse than I remembered.

Now there is the story of me
reading your story and the one
of you saying it
doesn't deserve such care.
I say it matters
that the dog stays by the chimney
for months, and a rain
soft as the sleep of cats
enters the land, emptied

of its cows, its wire gates pulled down
by hands that never dug
the single well, this whitened field.

I tried to write it out, to investigate the nature of vengeance, to disarm myself of the anger I carried. I wrote two poems about this event: "Two Stories" and "The Absence." Images from my uncle's death also appeared in "Stepping Outside," the title poem of my first, limited-edition collection. I began to see poems as a way of settling scores with the self. I felt I had reached the only possible justice for my uncle in the writing out of my anger and the honoring of the life that had been taken so brutally. The *In Cold Blood* aspect of my uncle's murder has caused violence to haunt my vision of what it is to live in America. Sometimes, with my eyes wide open, I still see the wall behind my grandfather's empty bed, and on it, the fiery angels and Jacob burning.

I felt if my uncle, the proverbial honest man, could be murdered in the middle of the night, then anything was possible. The intermittent hardships of my childhood were nothing compared to this. I saw how easily I could go into a state of fear and anger which would mar the energy of my life and consequently my poems for good. I think I began, in a steady way, to move toward accepting my own death, so that whenever it would come before me as a thought, I would release myself toward it. In the poems I've written that please me most, I seem able to see the experience with dead-living eyes, with a dead-living heart.

My own sense of time in poems approximates what I experience in my life—that important time junctures of past and present events via memory and actual presences are always inviting new meanings, revisions of old meanings, and speculation about things still in the future. These time shifts are a special province of poems because they can happen there more quickly, economically, and convincingly than in any other art form, including film. Film is still struggling to develop a language of interiority using the corporeal image, while even words like *drum* or *grief* in poems can borrow inflection from the overlap of words in context, can form whole new entities, as in a line from Louise Bogan's poem "Summer Wish": "the drum pitched deep as grief."

Since my intention here has been to emphasize experiential influences rather than literary ones, I must speak of the Vietnam War, for it was the war that finally caused me to take up my life as a poet. For the first time since I had left home for college, I was thrown back on my own resources. My husband and I had met when I was eighteen and married when I was twenty-one. I was twenty-six when he left to fly missions in Vietnam. I'd had very little life on my own. It became a time to test my strengths. I began working as a ward clerk in a hospital, on the medical floor. I did this for about five months, while the news of the war arrived daily in my mailbox. I was approaching what a friend of that time called an "eclipse." He urged me to leave the country. It was the best decision I could have made, as I look back now.

My time in Ireland and Europe during the Vietnam War put me firmly in possession of my own life. But in doing this, it made my life in that former time seem fraudulent. The returning veterans, my husband among them, had the hardship of realizing that many Americans felt the war to be wrong. This pervasive judgment was a burden to us both and one that eventually contributed to the dissolution of our marriage.

I began to experience a kind of psychic suffocation which expressed itself in poems that I copied fully composed from my dreams. For a while, this disassociation of dream material from my life caused the messages to go unheeded. But gradually my movement out of the marriage began to enact the images of dissolution in the poems. It was a parting that gave me unresolvable grief, yet at the same time allowed my life its first true joys as I began a full commitment to my writing. I think partings have often informed my poems with a backward longing, and it was especially so with this one.

I returned to Seattle in 1969 and began to study poetry with David Wagoner and Mark Strand at the University of Washington. My family did not understand what I was doing. Why should I divorce and then go back to college to learn to write poetry? It was beyond them. What was going to become of me now? Who would take care of me?

Trees have always been an important support to the solitude I connect with the writing of poetry. I suspect my affection and need of them began in those days in my childhood when I was logging with my parents. There was a coolness in the forest, a feeling of light filtering down from the arrow-shaped tops of the evergreens. The smell of pitch comes back. The chain-saw snarl and a spray of wood chips. Sawdust in the cuffs of my jeans. My brothers and I are again the woodcutter's children. We play under the trees, but even our play is a likeness to work. We construct shelters of rotten logs, thatch them with fireweed, and then invite our parents into the shelters to eat their lunches. We eat Spam sandwiches and smoked fish, with a Mountain Bar for dessert. After a time, my parents give me a little hatchet and a marking stick so I can work with them, notching the logs to be cut up into pulpwood to be made into paper. My brothers and I strip cones from the fallen trees, milking the hard pellets with our bare hands into gunnysacks, which are sold to the Forestry Department for ten dollars a bag. There is a living to be made and all of us are expected to do our share.

When I think of it now, it is not far from the building of those makeshift shelters to the making of poems. You take what you find, what comes naturally to the hand and mind. There was the sense with these shelters that they wouldn't last, but that they were exactly what could be done at the time. There were great gaps between the logs because we couldn't notch them into each other, but this allowed us to see the greater forest between them. It was a house that remembered its forest. And for me, the best poems, no matter how much order they make, have an undercurrent of forest, of the larger unknown.

To spend one's earliest days in a forest with a minimum of supervision gave a lot of time for exploring. I also had some practice in being lost. Both exploring and being lost are, it seems now, the best kind of training for a poet. When I think of those times I was lost, they come back with a strange exhilaration, as though I had died, yet had the possibility of coming back to life. The act of writing a poem is like that. It is that sense of aloneness which is trying to locate the world again, but not too soon, not until the voice has made its cry, "Here, here, over here," and the answering voices have called back, "Where are you?"

My mother and father started logging together in 1941, the year my mother traveled from Missouri by bus to marry my father. As far as she knows, she was the only woman who worked in the woods, doing the same work the men did. She was mainly the choker-setter and haul-back. She hauled the heavy steel cable, used to yard the logs into the landing, out over the underbrush to be hooked around the fallen trees. My mother's job was a dangerous one because the trees, like any dying thing, would often thrash up unexpectedly or re-lease underbrush which could take out an eye or lodge in one's side. She also lifted and stacked the pulpwood onto the truck and helped in the trimming of the branches. She did this work for seven years.

There is a photograph of my mother sitting atop two gi-gantic logs in her puffed-sleeve blouse and black work pants. It has always inspired me with a pride in my sex. I think I grew up with the idea that whatever the rest of the world said about women, the woman my mother was stood equal to any man and maybe one better. Her labor was not an effort to prove anything to anyone. It was what had to be done for the living. I did not think of her as unusual until I was about fourteen. I realized then that she was a wonderful mechanic. She could fix machines, could take them apart and reassem-ble them. None of the mothers of my friends had such faith in their own abilities. She was curious and she taught herself. She liked to tinker, to shift a situation or an object around. She had an eye for possibilities and a faculty for intuitive decision-making that afterward looked like knowledge. I feel I've transferred to the writing of poems many of my mother's explorative methods, even a similar audacity toward my materials.

"What happened to those letters?" I ask my mother over the telephone. I don't tell her I'm at the Dewitt Ranch Motel writing this essay. I don't tell her I'm trying to understand

My mother, Georgia Morris Bond, during the time she was logging with my father on Lost Mountain near Port Angeles, Washington, in 1951.

why I keep remembering my father's love letters as having an importance to my own writing.

"Well, a lot of them were sent to the draft board," she says. "Your dad and I were married November of forty-one. Pearl Harbor hit December seventh, so they were going to draft your father. A lot of men was just jumping up to get married to avoid the draft. We had to prove we'd been courting. The only way was to send the letters, so they could see for themselves."

"But what happened to the letters?"

"There was only about three of them left. You kids got into them, so I burnt them."

"You burnt them? Why? Why'd you do that?"

"They wasn't nothing in them."

"But you kept them," I say. "You saved them."

"I don't know why I did," she says. "They didn't amount to anything."

I hang up. I sit on one of the two beds and stare out at an identical arm of the motel which parallels the unit I'm in. I think of my father's love letters being perused by the members of the draft board. They become convinced that the courtship is authentic. They decide not to draft him into the war. As a result of his having written love letters, he does not go to his death, and my birth takes place. It is an intricate chain of events, about which I had no idea at the start of this essay.

I think of my father's love letters burning, of how they might never have come into their true importance had I not returned to them here in my own writing. I sit in the motel room, a place of much passage and no record, and feel I have made an important assault on the Great Nothing, though the letters are gone, though they did not truly exist until this writing, even for my parents, who wrote and received them.

My father's love letters are the sign of a long courtship and I pay homage to that, the idea of writing as proof of the courtship—the same blind, persistent hopefulness that carries me again and again into poems.

A Concert of Tenses
An Interview With Jeanie Thompson

Can you define your own poetry in terms of what you try to speak to, what your subjects are and also can you say what stylistic devices or special technical concerns are important to your poems?

That's incredible—the velocity of that question. I'll just start where I can. My subjects are taken from the events and people in my life. They reach community in the poems. Happenings and meetings that occurred years apart share a common space in the poem-life. The poem is then a place of pollination and cross-pollination for the actual. In this way it enlarges on the life. I would prefer to think that what was *fictional* in my life because of the separations caused by time stoppages and movements, becomes *real* again in the poems. I see them as a way of speaking toward people in my life who are mysterious and often cut off from me in an actual sense. I often speak into myself as one of these "missing persons," as if I were someone I used to know or am about to meet.

My sense of time is one of intersections where the past, present, and future are constantly interacting to produce a composite time. I'm trying to work with syntax in such a way as to almost create a verb tense in poetry which accommodates a faculty missing in the language as we use it daily. I'm searching for a verbal movement that is like a holograph.

This interview took place through the spring and summer of 1979. It was conducted by mail, over the phone, and ended with a meeting at Goddard College in Vermont.

This tense would allow you to approach yourself in a four dimensional way as everything you have been, are, and will be . . . through time. Maybe this could be called the "composite" tense.

I like the poems to reflect the ordinary, but with a sense of the natural mystery imbedded in all life, as though the boundary lines could be moved at any moment into our ghost lives, the accompaniment of that as eventuality. You find often I'll bring in the speaking voice of someone in the poems. It helps the population. Much of the quality of a life can be suggested quickly in a few gestures of the voice. My ear tunes in to the way people speak, the natural musicality of often the simplest expressions.

What you've called technical concerns only arise for me in the process of writing each poem. I've been writing at least two very different kinds of poems lately. One type is very lyrical and more moment-bound. The other extends into prose territory, I suppose. The language is a little less heightened, the rhythms lankier, the tone more contemplative and open to incident, a higher mix of randomness affecting the attention of the poem.

I think my endings tend to startle readers. That might be an identifiable technical trait of mine, that the endings are allowed to rise to some peak of emotion that contemporary writers think unfashionable, as if we haven't a right to our own passions and should taper off and be noncommital in order to sneak up on a truth. There's something to that, but I want to work with my natural inclination, rushing the language into the experience until it overspills from the sheer impetus and urgency of the voice. I've always been struck by endings that fix a moment irrevocably in the memory, endings like Louise Bogan's, a line like "The thin hound's body arched against the snow," which is a very rich image to try and pull off these days. Too poised really for current taste.

How can you defend your poems against the charge that the line breaks or stanza patterns often seem arbitrary or quirky? Although I'm playing the devil's advocate here, it is a charge that we all know is leveled against contemporary poetry by formalists, or those only used

*to the comfort of recognizable forms, and also by some who enjoy free
verse but find no apparent reason for many contemporary poets' line
breaks and stanza breaks.*

I remember a party after a reading in Cincinnati where I had
to do exactly that with a group of readers. They asked me to
justify the breaks. We sat on the floor and went over the
poems. For all that can be said about reasons, though, where
you break the line is still highly instinctual, a kind of balance
you're keeping between eye and ear and meaning. It's a study
in attention and emphasis really, when you go through a
poet's work noticing where the lines break, where the stanzas
end or impel you into the next small arena of experience. I
like a sense of expectancy and tend to stop the line before it
answers itself. Same thing for stanzas. You'll often have to
jump with me as though the white space between stanzas were
there to make you wonder about "next."

Still, I don't like to irritate the reader or be tricky. I do want
to get all the positive ambiguity I can out of the line as a unit
of movement so I pay attention to that when I break.

What are the major stylistic differences between Instructions to the
Double *and* Under Stars? *It's apparent that one of your main
subjects in all your poems is other people—your caring for them,
though not to the exclusion of or effacement of self. But I see a change
in tone/style from first to second book.* Under Stars *seems more
lyrical, more quiet, sometimes wistful, and more self-assured. I guess
what I'm saying is that the subjects seem to me to be ongoing, but the
style seems to have mellowed.*

A prominent magazine editor in speaking to me about a
young woman poet I'd admired said he didn't like her second
book because she'd mellowed too much after having a baby,
so I cringe a little at the word "mellowed." I haven't had
babies, but I seem to have arrived at some process of reaching
emotional and spiritual equilibrium which accommodates loss
without denying its very consequences. That is, I haven't
stopped feeling anguish for the hard truths—that people we
love do die or lose faith in us and themselves, that there are

regrets which will never be solved, which hold us prisoner. But I know now this isn't all.

I still respect the urgencies of that first book of mine. Some irreparable damage had been done to the terrain of my life. My uncle, one of three central figures in my life at that time, had been murdered in the middle of the night. My first marriage had failed under the stresses of the Vietnam War. Like many women I suddenly saw all the people I hadn't been and could never have hoped to be because of the indentured status of women in this country. I found myself looking into those differences I was raised with, having grown up with three brothers. I was realizing all those lost promises and aware of my own part in causing my apartness. There was a lot of anxiety. I was mapping out some very serious uncharted territory. You go a long way in a life before you see that the possibilities were limited by factors often beyond your control. You don't want to fall into a self-sorry attitude or into anger, nor can you travel far on undaunted hopefulness.

The voice in *Under Stars,* to my way of thinking, is very practical and head-on at times ("On Your Own," "3 A.M. Kitchen: My Father Talking," "Poem Written Near a Candle") and at other times it's very thoughtful, as if considering a spectrum of alternatives. *Spectrum,* that's an important word to me. My thinking belongs more to the spectrum now, less to the target. That means the contours of the poems will be more adaptable perhaps, less insistent toward answers or arrivals of the sort I might have headed toward in the first book. Even the title, *Instructions to the Double,* reflects the strictures I was feeling then. These still exist, only I regard them differently now. For one thing, I express the ironies with more self-humor, I think, though readers seem to have trouble catching my humor. It does inform the voice in *Under Stars,* especially in poems like "If Never Again" and "Ever After."

The self-assurance you mention feeling is just a product of being able to recover better both in the life and the art, with less rancor and more enterprise. That's what it is to be creative.

John Ashbery says somewhere that his most important literary influence was the sound of his mother's voice. What were some of your primary literary influences?

The Bible was the only book in our house for most of my childhood. Then I found *The Jungle Book* in a drawer where I thought it had been hidden from us. It was like a secret in green covers I kept taking out and entering without arrival. That boy raised by wolves was an early companion, along with the boy David. Then Joseph, Bethsheba, Jesus, and all that great cast of the Bible.

My grandfather used to sing to me in Missouri. He had a team of horses named Dolly and Daisey he plowed with. These were probably the best serenaded horses of the century. I sang with him. Maybe it was important to sing to horses. Who can say? They were so patient with bad voices singing to them about Jessie James and Pretty Redwing while they did all the work. The motion of their necks nodding ahead of us on the wagon, I still remember it. Now, Irish traditional songs are one of the most important influences on my poems. They have ways of haunting the ordinary, and my taste for them was probably set in childhood.

From the time I was five until I was fifteen I played classical piano. I read the lives of Beethoven, Bach, Chopin, and Mozart. I played their music until my hands knew the pieces by heart. This gave me a sense of form, of melody and accompaniment, of rhythm, of themes, of risings and fallings, of emotion carried by time.

Then you also see other things besides "literature" as "literary influences"?

Certainly there are important influences other than literary. I mean, is John Ashbery's mother's voice literary? Maybe it's more interesting to speak of these nonliterary influences because they're the most individual.

My brothers and I played in the woods while my mother and father worked at logging in a clearing nearby. We built shelters out of fireweed and small trees. Out of what was at hand. Then we would invite my parents into these at lunch-time. We ate Spam sandwiches on white bread. There was the smell of pitch and sawdust. It was very important to build those houses together for our parents who were working hard. Later I was given a little hatchet with which to trim the trees before they were sawed into pulpwood. I remember feeling very important. I had a thing to do. I was helping to earn the living. The days were musical, punctuated by the occasional falling of a tree, the silences between a furor of chainsaw activity. Sometimes we got lost and had to find our way back to the road or the clearing through the timber. I used to imagine that our parents might go off and leave us one day like the woodcutter in Hansel and Gretel. We seemed to be in a kind of training for that day when we would have to live off blackcaps and salmon berries like the bears. All of this has everything to do with my poems, a tone of self-sufficiency with an appreciation for sacrifices and hard work, the close-ness of family, its heartaches and tenderness.

Roethke was an early teacher, but before that, Margaret Matthieu taught me. She was my high school English teacher. She had us read poetry in the *Atlantic Monthly*. I don't know who wrote it or what it was about, but a poem I read there in 1961 changed my life. I wasn't ready for Roethke so I'm only understanding now things that were said to me when I was eighteen. I got a love of Yeats from him that has been my strongest influence in a constant way. I know a lot of him by heart and his *Collected Poems* are always in my suitcase.

I found a series of opposites or contraries in "The Ireland Poems" series of Under Stars *and made a list of them. Two of them are:*

> . . . There is a woman
> beside me, younger, older, waving
> as you are waving yet,
> with your blonde hair
> wound and pinned, into this distance.
>
> ("Still Moment at Dun Laoghaire")

> . . . the perfect map
> of this return where I have met
> and lost you willingly
> in a dead and living place.
> > ("Disappearances in the Guarded Sector")

What are you attempting to do with this method—is it special to Ireland or is it part of a larger concern?

I think the places in your life where you feel contradictory tensions, yet a rightness or at least intrigue with the way the opposites balance each other into stasis, are fertile moments for the poet. A secret lives there, and although you don't want to solve it really, you instinctually want to mark your recognition of those forces answering one another so curiously. It's probably a variation on my double theme, these opposites fulfilling each other.

Balance in one's life is so attitudinal. You surrender a lot of living to the negative side of the ledger if you can't find the positive in the negative. I don't mean in any cheap, self-satisfied way, but in a way that the opposites do truthfully include the possibility of the joint perspective. I wrote a line in "Poem Written Near a Candle" that might show what I mean. I say "Nettles could be feathers / the moment they brush your / ankle." You see I've found an instance of truth that upsets your fixed notions about both nettles and feathers, so that their attributes partake of one another. I've effected the imagined nature of these elements and on a metaphorical level I've reminded myself of those moments in which the dangerous or repellent elements are easily capable of the sensual attributes of benign and elegant signs like feathers.

Now that you ask, it does occur to me that Ireland, especially the North, was full of such contradictory elements that it probably did draw forth more of this kind of motion from me. With the violence in the North there is a closeness among one's immediate friends that I found very paradoxical. There are small pockets of inclusiveness and protectiveness, then enormous disparities outside those. The kind of oppression that the Irish Catholics feel constantly in so many ways promotes a spiritual overflow in the traditional Irish music scene, for instance. The way in which music preserves the memory of the struggles has such obvious power as a revolutionary force, especially since music seems benign, as something meant only to please the senses, yet it is also a form of living history in the songs and in the passing down of the tunes from musician to musician. Poetry, since it happens in words alone, is perhaps too bald an art in a country where you could be shot for a wrong opinion. It's hard to write a poetry that could accommodate the past and present of Ireland. The music I've heard there has a spiritual fullness I find lacking in much of the poetry I've read there. This power of music is an oasis in a country of so many fears. These fragile sounds of the air are such a paradoxical kind of strength.

I do see the double still at work in Under Stars. *Although I think it permeates the book, I sense it distinctly, for instance, in "Ever After," and "The Sky Behind It." Is it essential for you to work through a doubling process of self or personality or a splitting of self in order to achieve a wholeness?*

Yes, this is just what I'm doing, but not so much a "splitting" as re-creating by formulation of opposing or self-inclusive personae.

The double in *Instructions to the Double* was a way of speaking into the self. I was acknowledging the specific challenge of being a woman in my time, of growing up with one set of expectations (children, marriage, home) and then adding to this the expectations of the feminist movement (career, self-sufficiency, movement away from secondary fulfillment in children and male partners). Even if you don't agree with some of the overtones of the feminist movement (the constant self-first focus, for example) you are still pervasively affected. . . . I think I used this "double" voice to antagonize some aspects of my womanhood, the temptress aspect for instance, the constant sufferer, the "little mother" self that feels it has to run around taking care of everybody and his goat.

The double in my first book was used to acknowledge the

exclusions and failures of the womanhood I had lived so far, and when I say womanhood I mean the woman who lives with dignity and fulfillment within the community, not the one who stands on the hillock and cries king of the mountain. When my woman in "The Woman Who Raised Goats" has to raise goats and then confide in them and then suffer her clothes to be eaten by them while her brothers play cards in the hiring hall, this is a dramatization of the sort of exclusion I'm talking about, the kind women live—doing two-thirds of the world's work and receiving one-tenth of its pay—that sort of inequity.

When in "The Likeness" the woman reveals the breast she has scarred to keep her man, it is at once an admission of dreadful need and the will to self-abnegation and degradation. She takes pleasure in her scar, the palpable sign of her deeper psychic or spiritual injury. The speaker, unlike her, wears the sign internally with no visible sign. She is caught in a numbness, a hideous stasis.

In *Under Stars* the double in the poem you mention, "Ever After," is more invitational, more of an accompaniment than an exclusion. The speaker is a dead woman speaking to the woman who has just recently been buried beside her. She has moments of humor about her own death and then she begins to advise the newcomer about the state she is entering. If these presences are seen as aspects of each other then you begin to witness a welcoming of the self at the point where the speaker says: "If I were everything, there would be nothing / beside me. You / are beside me." This "beside" characteristic is an expression of self-equality, perhaps, of helpmate closeness.

In "The Sky Behind It" there's a voyeuristic quality to the double, a self-watching capacity, and the enactment is one of foreboding as though the self were a living ghost, a haunting of the real. A house must be entered. It is empty: "You / let yourself in. You do." So again, the self takes its own initiative toward the unpopulated area. In "My Mother Remembers She Was Beautiful" the daughter uses the figure of the mother's young and adult beauty to draw questions about the denials and legacies and the abandonments one suffers as a woman with or without beauty. The poem ends on the beauty of snow over houses, "the brave and wondering lights of the houses." "Still Moment at Dun Laoghaire" is another of these shared identity poems where two sisters realize they have a language between them in their absent, yet very present, childhood.

I'm curious about the person addressed in "Your Letter is Being Written Without You"; it seems that we know a lot about the speaker by way of the "you" but that it's in fact almost impossible to know who the "you" is. Are we supposed to know, or are there "shared identities" here, too?

It's a "you" that often acts as a double for the speaking voice, then widens to include the reader as "you" and carries both speaker and reader into the concern for a specific "you." It's best to read this poem with a loose rein, without trying to pin the "you" down. It keeps trying you on and perhaps it's annoying to end up as somebody else when you realize the "you" is probably someone I knew in my childhood. I was working toward an intimacy in the voice that could break out of the purely personal, yet include it and enlarge it, the way it could be serious to be remembered in someone else's childhood. We are all mythically alive out there as the memory of someone who's gone on without us. That's why the "you" keeps abandoning the reader, then focusing in to specifics like the heart-murmur girl or to the direct address at the end, "Mr. Sad-to-say." I did have a specific man in mind when I began the poem, but he became a character and the poem outgrew him.

Do you always see being "on your own" the way you do in the poem of that name? Especially in the last stanza?

> It's like this on your own: The charms
> unlucky, the employment
> solitary, the best love always
> the benefit of a strenuous doubt.

I suppose you're getting at the idea that this is a bit harsh as a view, but sometimes things that are harsh are also true. But no, "always" is a long time and I don't always see being on your own like this. But mostly, for sure. It's a very exposed position, being a woman alone. If I were a woman alone with children, I'd have written this even more strongly. I saw a woman carrying one child and moving around a table in an airport to feed two others. Then she tried to carry a metal baby chair over to the table. The man at my table got up to help her. She seemed surprised. "Thank you," she said. "You learn to do a lot of things with one arm." She was still carrying the baby.

I've liked the solitariness of being alone. I get a lot done. Whole days of thinking and dreaming, reading and writing. I'm good for others after this sort of time. There's a great pleasure in sharing, and in daily sharing with even one other. You have to think of someone besides yourself and that's a goodness. When good things happen there's someone to celebrate with. If a hardship comes, there's the comfort and aid of the other. Having lived long periods without this, I feel the richness of a right companionship. In the life alone, it's a talent to keep yourself from feeling left out and sad. I've got that as reserve. Face it. Most women are going to end up alone with themselves, or with each other, the life span of men being what it is. All you have to do is visit an old folks' home to know that women are going to have to love the company of women in the final days. Denise Levertov wrote a wonderful poem called "Woman Alone" which says it better than I can.

How important is travel to your work?

I'm typing the answer to this on the Edmonds ferry boat to Port Townsend, Washington, on Father's Day. Earlier I was typing in the car to help you meet the deadline and because I had thoughts toward your questions that I wanted to get out before they got overclear and left me behind. Travel in this instance is a bit frustrating. I often have to be in movement in cars or on airplanes when I'd rather be sitting in a room at a desk. You have to get inventive. Think what you can do in those spaces most people waste. I do a lot of my correspondence in the air so that the times when I'm near a desk can go to the poems.

As you know, I wrote about half of my last book in Ireland. My ambition in writing those poems was not to exclude the reader who hasn't been there, but to approach the particular scene in such a way that it maintains its Irishness without losing its appeal to lives anywhere, the anywhere of America. Poems written outside the country often become travelogues and I wanted to avoid that, get back to the common ground of people everywhere and the differences of the Irish people I met. It was important to encounter myself as American, and the only way to do that in a living way is to immerse yourself in another culture, to find the aspects of your viewpoint which aren't absorbed, which cause your difference.

When you visit Ireland as an American woman poet, how are you received? What is most valuable to you and your work about that experience? You said in New Orleans that poets in Ireland are not as obsessive about poetry as poets in America are, and also that the level of wit in conversations is very high, infectious. Do you care to say more about that?

I'm just now, after three years from that first visit to the poets in Northern Ireland, beginning to glimpse my reception. The Irish are so hospitable that you mistake at first their reception of you as a person for their reception of your work. During this last trip I was told by my best friend that he'd really had to argue for my poetry there, that the poets there just weren't convinced that my writing was any good. You see, they have to shift a lot of very deep values just to approach American poetry. Many Irish poets are still interested in rhyme and a stricter use of meter, things that make them seem antiquated to an American poet, but things which remind us of that long tradition in English poetry. You have to think seriously of this all again when you go to Ireland. You can't dismiss it as easily as Robert Bly did in the seventies when he advised American poets that they could proceed or *should* proceed on their own ground and forget English poetry. This was probably a very necessary thing to get said in the late fifties, early sixties. But now it seems like an overstatement.

My view of poetry has been very much enriched for the trouble I've taken to establish a living relationship to Irish and English contemporary and modern poetry—the whole tradition of poetry in English, for that matter. I have a good idea of what's been done and how it relates to contemporary interests in America.

I see that I've overlooked that word "woman" in your question. . . . My womanhood is one aspect of my being. It certainly made me a curiosity on the Irish scene. You just don't meet many Irish women poets. There are only two that you hear about in conversation and I haven't heard a kind word about either from the men poets. Their remarks have had little to do with the poetry of these women, but are more personal jibes as to whether or not they're pretty. One is Eavan Boland and Eiléan Ni Chuilleanáin is the other. Boland is seen as being the Irish version of Sylvia Plath. She adopts some of the tone perhaps but the style is more toward Bogan, that tight rein and the images in bold relief, feeling their special significance as they're offered. Ni Chuilleanáin has an American publisher and comes much closer to American taste, the form on the page untidy like our own and the voice heading closer to the personal. I have since come to see that my ease with the Irish male poets probably comes from the fact that I'm not going to stay in Ireland. They don't have to compete with me. So they can afford to be generous. As they mean to be.

One of the things about my being an American poet which struck my listeners in Ireland in 1976 was that I was personal and also I was a woman speaking personally in a country where women were just beginning to speak at all. It made the women very shy of me. They would hardly come up to speak to me after the readings, though I felt they wanted to and after a period of awkwardness I began to move toward them to bridge the silence.

The poetry scene, like the traditional Irish music scene in Ireland, is still almost totally a male scene. I get along well with the men and feel included by them. They want to hear me, to talk to me and have become gradually more open to what I'm doing, though we argue a lot about it. They don't like the discursive trend in American poetry, think the shortest way to saying something is always the best, something which has recently come into doubt even more strongly via Ashbery in this country. They don't trust the way American poetry bends all experience so deeply into the personal and this reaction has definitely affected me, made me want to find a broader way of employing the intimacy that the personal voice has afforded us.

As I said to you when we met in New Orleans, it was a great relief to get out of the obsessive American poetry scene. To meet poets who talked about other things besides poetry. Poetry there means what it should mean, being generously open to a broad scope of life experience. The poets in Ireland know how to entertain one another, to tell stories, to sing, to give the history of the place they're standing in.

You mention Irish wit, and this is one thing I get very homesick for when I leave Ireland. Wit is contagious. Your mind and mouth begin to work that way when you're in conversation where it's a mode of relating. There's a preciseness you get in Irish wit that we don't meet often in America. Here conversation is often a series of incompletions, thoughts trailing off. In Irish conversation there's always the surprise of a moment of wit punctuating what seemed, for a moment, matter of fact. This moment is like a basketball being carried over the heads of the players toward the basket, then everyone struggles to tip it in again and again until a kind of relief breaks through into laughter or an unanswerable silence. It's essentially play and very invigorating for someone who loves to see language put through its paces.

In all your traveling, do you feel the need for a home or a place of some specific locale to call yours, to which you can always return?

I don't lack places to call home, but I do need a central place from which to venture out. So far I live in a state of constant returnings so as to preserve a sense of belonging to my home area of the Olympic Peninsula in Washington State. I've also become so close to the poets and musicians I met in Ireland that I've felt compelled to go back there each year since 1976 for some period of time. There's no getting around it; you have to go to a place to deserve its belonging, though certainly you carry much of any loved place with you when you're away.

I've had to work one-year jobs at universities away from the Northwest for the past several years. You begin to want a more steady location in this "away" life too at this stage. As a friend said to me in Seattle recently: "Isn't it something, that you get to spend so little time with the people you love most." It's this way with places in my life.

I know one of your main interests besides poetry is film. I have a sense of a cinematic eye in Instructions to the Double *and also in* Under Stars—*almost as if you were setting scenes, though I don't mean that in a pejorative way at all. I'm thinking particularly of "Time Lapse with Tulips," and "Crossing" from* Instructions to the Double, *and from* Under Stars *the ending of "Second Language." There's also the image of the face flickering on the train window, the tunnel's darkness, and the sudden burst of light in "Open Fire Near a Shed" and also the first line of "Woman Enough": "Figures on a silent screen." Do you make conscious crossings from film to poetry (or vice versa)?*

It's just a natural outgrowth of my filmmaking and film-watching. Even now when I carry a Super-8 camera around with me it attracts me to certain qualities of light, to movements and points of view I wouldn't think of otherwise. In a poem from *Instructions to the Double* called "Croce e Delizia al Cor" I take the point of view of a camera held by someone in a swing facing the ocean and a picket fence. This camera-as-eye technique was first used by the French Impressionist film-makers back in the mid-1920s, before sound. They were lashing their cameras to cowcatchers, bicycles, and other moving objects so that suddenly you could see the train tracks as a train would see it. Those shocks of light in "Open Fire Near a Shed" are familiar to us as an image cameras have given us in the movies when we go through the tunnel on the train and suddenly break out into pastureland and light. Then I can go, as a camera can, into the close-up of cows breathing over the tracks of birds.

But films have most influenced my Time-sense. In the cutting room I like snipping away all but the essential gestures, quickening some action into interest or so that it feeds into the next motion in a satisfying way. Large blocks of time can be moved ahead of things that actually happened later, thereby giving them suspense so you wait to learn their causes. I can also stay with a simple action, like raising an axe over one's head before striking a block of wood, until it seems slower than it happens and you pay attention to it newly. I make jump-cuts in my poems just like films do, too. I think some of my speakers talk as though they were being watched by cameras—take the voice in "You Talk on Your Telephone; I Talk on Mine" when it asks, "Are they filming this?"

My Irish friend, Ciarán Carson, said he felt like he was in a movie the entire time he was first in America because so much of what he knew of America came from films. This is true for those of us who live here too, I think! The way life as perceived in movies is a pervasive force. I'd like to write an essay about this, on the relationship of filmic images to images and techniques in contemporary poetry.

As a poet, what part does fiction play in your life and work?

I've always loved reading nonfiction—books about survivals in the Antarctic or the life of Chagall or Emily Dickinson's letters or the book on the lives of our cells. Short stories are the sort of fiction I like best. I've gotten back to fiction since my stay in Missoula where I knew so many fine fiction writers—Bill Kittridge, Rick De Marinis, Jim Crumley, Jim Welch. Reading their books was a part of knowing them. I had written stories from 1969 to 1972. But when I went to Iowa to the Writers' Workshop I turned to poetry and film. The sort of time I had available for reading and writing must have changed.

My temperament in language has quickened incredibly

through working in poetry. I often can't bear how long it takes to set up a scene in prose. I can do it in three lines in a poem, so I get impatient with prose. My interior clock, the one that reminds me I have a death to meet, is in steady alarm some days. I can't do enough quickly enough. Even when I write just a few lines I'm often compelled by this time urgency. The fiction writer feels this less, in my experience. I would love to rediscover that ease.

I recently shut myself up for four days and wrote a twenty-page short story. Ray Carver has been an inspiration to me. He writes so well you can read him aloud. Many fiction writers' books can't hold up under that. The attention lets go. When I read popular fiction, even a book which has gotten some literary acclaim, I often say to myself, "You could do as well as that," and then I think, "But you don't admire that." So I don't feel challenged or enlivened enough to write fiction. Until now. You see, I read Conrad in 1970 and I felt I had to be as fine a writer as that. So I just closed up. I mean, in my own mind, my own way, I had to write as inventively and with as much dimension as Conrad. Lately, when I read Flannery O'Connor or Carver I believe in the power of fiction again and the power of the short story—that it is capable of being lyrical like the poem, but also that it's able to include all the paraphernalia of life and to give the sense of conversation, of people in a dialogue which is going to change them.

Do you see the interview or the book review as a critical endeavor? By that I mean how do they instruct you?

In the interview you're really overhearing the poet gossip with someone who has an intelligent interest in the attitudes of the poet. These attitudes may even influence contemporary readings of the poems for those who happen to read the poems, either before or after the interview. I call it "gossip," because most of the poem's life comes to it through its own powers as a verbal organism in the lives of others whose imaginations may be touched by words in a certain orchestration. What I say of what I do may make *me* look silly but the poem will have nothing to do with me in that event. I happen to enjoy gossip. We often say things to make ourselves more interesting, things that are exaggerated for emphasis or to cause our listener's eyebrows to rise. A little disapproval enlivens things. Gossip is attached to the personality of the writer and is therefore more like a kind of atmosphere in which the work got done, often miraculously. It's a kind of weather vane but its winds are fickle. Interviews are most interesting to me as a subject when the interviewer knows my work and we don't have to discover my favorite color. In these informed cases, the questions of the interviewer indicate critical questions that perplex the reader, and I'm very much interested in these because I often learn what confuses readers or hurts reception of the experiences—even as the reader adds his/her own riches to the poem. I have to listen to see whether the reader failed the possibilities the poem presented or whether it was me—not giving a clear or worthwhile path.

The book review is too brief usually to do more than offer a few tantalizing or swift judgments. If you don't know what informs the reviewer's taste it's hard to gauge his/her opinions. Your book may get favorable or unfavorable comment due to the company it keeps in the review, comparisons that happen just because your book is born at the same time as others. Reviews often tend to deal only with the "new" book on its own without full reference to previous work. The book reviews I like to read are those that express preference in a way that piques my curiosity. I often learn what appeals to a reader and I have to say to myself: "Do I want to please that sort of reader in that way?"

The first national review I got was awful. In the *New York Times*. It looked at my first book, *Instructions to the Double*, as a feminist document. I knew the reviewer, a man, had perhaps read the title poem and skimmed the rest. He was reacting, not reading. He didn't like my seriousness, advised me to develop a sense of humor. I was actually very humbled by these opinions at the time they hit. Some judgment that was accompanying me all along had suddenly and violently intersected my life. Even if the opinion is good, as it has been more often than not in my case, it comes as a kind of violence to one's life. Your work begins (through the opinions of the review) to act upon you, instead of your acting upon it as in its creation.

Perhaps it's only now I'm answering that long-ago reviewer with more humor in the poems, but not because he asked. My life now just allows more humor. Humor is a survival mechanism, but it also means you're at ease enough in your life that you have the leisure of showing enjoyment. I'd had quite a few hard life events which give impetus to many of the poems in my first book. Maybe developing a sense of humor only happens in one's thirties—like the awful sense of what American society expects of women hits you hardest in your mid-thirties, because the first signs of aging begin in earnest. I still feel that reviewer's need for humor was as limiting as my lack of it. People ask quite a lot of a poet these days. They seem to want every poem to be an orchestra when sometimes you wanted only to hear a sad melody played on the flute.

Are you bothered by the prospect of a critic "explicating" your poems? I heard a poet say recently that if she thought some person were going to make money, after her death, by telling what her poems meant or were about, she would write it all herself before she died to prevent such a thing from happening. Since she made that remark I've wondered how other poets feel about that.

I don't feel that I'm the central authority of my poems, so this causes me to regard them less jealously. No, it doesn't bother me to find others are thinking they know what I meant. That's the point, really.

Unlike many poets, I find criticism very interesting. On occasion I learn something and am grateful. It is a pity that critics can make more money from talking about poems than the poets can themselves, perhaps. But who said the world was fair? You do what you can, of course, in your own small corner to try to make it so, to make it fair.

The term "formal criticism" makes me remember my first encounter with the word "formal," which was one of those silk or taffeta dresses, low-cut to show what little cleavage you had. You put this on to go to the big dance of the year in your high school. You were on show and moved like an object full of potential disaster. Formal criticism is a lot like this. Slow moving and always *verging* on actually saying something. I enjoy even this awkwardness about it at times, this sense that it has been dressed up for an occasion. The Irish have a wonderful saying: "Beware of occasions which demand new clothes." This is a warning that one's true and honest bearing in the world may be made inappropriate by an occasion which asks you to appear as anyone other than yourself. Critics are under this terrible pressure of new clothes I think.

Many poets, on the other hand, are superstitious about learning what images they repeat or what verbal tense or tone or subject they persistently use. There's always distortion in the critical view and this often puts poets off. For me it's like a mirror I met continually in my childhood at the family shoe store. I could get fat or thin or normal according to how I placed myself in front of it; my location caused the view. It was a curiosity to me. Even distortions are a form of truth, but you have to keep recognition of your own form and person in mind as it lives in the poems when you look into the critic's ideas about what you've done. The discrepancies can be very enlightening.

You told me recently that you were both surprised and pleased when Peter Davison in reviewing Under Stars (Atlantic Monthly, *June, 1979), appeared to understand the way you are working with time in those poems.*

Well, I was surprised about Peter Davison's review because I didn't know anyone but me had been aware of my wanting to write with all the tenses and doing that regularly in this last book. I've begun to watch for how other poets handle time, and I realize other poets are also doing this some of the time, even if they don't use it as a central technique as I do. One poet centrally concerned with time is Yehuda Amichai. In fact, his new book is entitled *Time*. It's one long, beautiful poem which is testing the boundaries. Other poets do it in lines, get that composite sense of time I was talking about earlier. I'm thinking just now of a poem of Dick Hugo's in the anthology *A Geography of Poets* called "Places and Ways to

Live," in which he writes a line with the kind of velocity and time-sense I aspire to: "The dark came early / in that home, came early for the last time soon." I like how the past funnels down into a present which has the finality of a past, yet poses expectation in that word "soon."

I really don't think of what I'm trying to accomplish in any programmatic sense as regards time in my poems. Each poem has its own problems and excitements and I'm really waiting for the full range of those demands to be asked of me as I work. I expect I'll continue the syntactical strategies, also the use of incidental past moments to inform the present. I just want to write so the full concert of tenses corresponds to my personal vision of our lives in time, the mystery of that.

Poetry in Translation
Literary Imperialism or, Defending the Musk Ox

With so much poetry now available in translation, it is not surprising that those of us who have little or no knowledge of other languages are having a hard time deciding what a good translation is. A few years back, a colleague of mine at the University of Montana suggested to me that perhaps "the moron's point of view," as she put it, ought to be represented.

Perhaps it's only right then, in the high spirit of adventure afoot in the field of translation in America now, that I should attempt to speak about translation, having at hand only the one language I was born to—a longshoreman's variant of English on my father's side and my mother's Missouri Ozark inflection on the other.

Poetry is the only second language I'm ever likely to have or that will have me in the full way a language possesses its native speaker. And there is the sense, in speaking of translation, in which all poems are a form of translation, the carrying of a secret inner cargo into visible harbors for the use, comfort, and sometimes mystification of those faraway islanders one is not permitted to meet face to face—but upon whom one may nevertheless have a lasting and often nourishing effect. In the making of the poem, the poet's inner language finds an external form. Or very often, the opposite is true: the poet's external world (I make the distinction faithlessly for the point) is translated into emotional or internal terms.

But in its most matter-of-fact sense, the word *translation* indicates the carrying over of words in one language into the facsimile of meaning in a second language. In the translation of poetry it's obvious that there is an extreme violence inherent in this act, since poetry depends so much on sound and rhythms for its impact, not to say "meanings." A comprehensive discussion of this dilemma by Charles Tomlinson appears in his introduction to *The New Oxford Book of Verse in English Translation* (1980). He begins by quoting Rossetti's dictum that, at the very least, "a good poem shall not be turned into a bad one." This ambition is a necessity and, indeed, those of us who can't compare the original to the translation with any sense of accuracy *do* depend on the translated poem to be a good poem in the English it has come to. So wherever the poem started, what an English-only reader wants is a good poem in English.

What more should the translator do? There seems to be a consensus of opinion among the poet-translators Tomlinson quotes that the translator is there to preserve the "flame" of the poet's *intent* and not the "ashes" of the original form— these images are taken from Dryden's criticism of those translators who stick too closely to the text and his corresponding applause for those who honor the spirit of the text:

> They but preserve the Ashes, thou the Flame,
> True to his sense, but truer to his fame.

Tomlinson also cites Sir John Denham's belief that an irreplaceable loss would take place unless the translator could add a new spirit to the emerging text. Dryden, whom Tomlinson identifies as the greatest translator of all times, favors keeping the sense of the words, and this sense could be "amplified, but not altered." Donald Davie approves translation which "takes more liberties than the 'trot,' but denies itself the liberties of the imitation and of other relations more tenuous still."

These "other relations" to the word "translation" give evidence of the variety of approaches various poets and translators have taken toward bringing the poem over into the new language. I made a brief list from Tomlinson's introduction of the terms used to indicate these alternate routes: "adaptation," "imitation," "paraphrase," "translation with latitude," and "creative translation." From a collection of papers delivered by translators at the Conference on Literary Translation held in New York in May, 1970, I compiled another list which gives clues to the ambitions of various translators: "recreating," "transmitting," "renovation," "bringing up to date," "evocation," and even a call for "connivance and complicity" in translating.

The latitude evidenced in these lists suggests that translation aspires to telepathy on the one hand and the stance of a benevolent dictator on the other. It is hard for a monolingual reader to know what to trust in a translation when one realizes that the poet-translator has often been working from a paraphrased version ("trot") of the text, which has been written out by a native speaker for the translator from a language the translator does not know. What the reader gets in this case is a translation of a translation. Perhaps this is not as strong an argument against accuracy as it may seem when we realize that during World War II the head of the American Cryptoanalytic Section of the Army Intelligence decoded the Japanese diplomatic code without knowing Japanese. Hayden Carruth has commented on this briefly:

> This (the decoding of a message without knowledge of the originating language) is regarded by the uninformed as an impossible feat. But the code is itself a language, with referents that can be (approximately, very approximately) identified with particular elements of reality which exist in both Japan and the U.S.A. The same with a poem. Except that a poem, being imagined, may be somewhat more untranslatable, or difficult to assimilate to cultural preconceptions, than a military message (or a work of prose fiction).

Accordingly, if the poet does not know the language the poem has been translated from, all may yet go well if the poet is intuitionally attuned to the unknown language and able to decode it in this manner. As Carruth seems to admit, this may be possible for translating messages, but for poetry or fiction in which the texture of the language is more than informational, this decoding without knowledge of the originating language would result in the barest of scaffolds.

The translator, then, can be any or all combinations of pirate, cannibal, smuggler, extortionist, and lover. He's even a kind of blind bureaucrat of the soul. Stanley Kunitz says translating is like reconstructing a ruined city, and this seems to have heroic overtones. If we go a step further and call translating a form of urban renewal, we are, however, reminded of the terrible cost in terms of the character of once highly individualized neighborhoods—the homogenization, the sometimes misdirected efforts at making an area "presentable." Similarly, one suspects that much is lost in the move to make the translation "presentable" in the new language. The danger, then—and often the certainty—is that the translator has had to over-civilize the poem. There's the opposite danger, of course, of the translator who knows the language with such intimacy that he's likely to turn the poem into an artifact of ruthless exactitude. Or he may present some incredible amputee by forgetting to whisper a few sweet-nothings. He may even produce, God forbid, an outerspace mutant, so rich in possibility that it waddles through the doorway on fourteen legs, wearing a head like a fire hydrant.

The most convincing way of avoiding the mutant effect of translation may be Pound's suggestion that the translator be able to integrate the qualities and combinations of energy rather than merely the words themselves. The translator must find a way of arranging his substituted words, says Tomlinson, so that *"the electric current flows and that there is no current wasted."* This idea of maintaining the current of energy in the translation appeals to me, but how is someone who doesn't know both languages to know whether this current has been maintained or not? Simple, says a friend of mine teaching in a French department: get someone who knows the language to read the poem in the language it was translated from and tell you. This would be fine, if I could find this willing translator, and if he or she had expertise in poetry. All too often, the poem appears only in English (acknowledging a lack of interest in the original version?), so an original of the poem must be sought first. Also, if I want to read an anthology of translations conscientiously, I must assemble my own United Nations.

Elsa Gress in "The Art of Translating" says that it takes "both literary and linguistic know-how to evaluate the essential qualities in a translation to see whether a tone has been rendered or not, and whether tricky problems have been solved or left unsolved." Thus, it is not enough to find someone who has a working knowledge of the language; this translator-friend must also be able to assess tone. Perhaps it would not hurt if this translator were also a poet. The range of those qualified begins to narrow.

All this does not inspire confidence that the reader with only English at his disposal will be able to recognize the superior or even the good translation. Perhaps the one recourse such a reader has is to read the arguments for and against the various translations as they are reviewed—if indeed they are reviewed. Aside from this, one may line up various translations of the same poem by various translators and try to see which translation prevails as a good poem in English while it *seems* to carry a quality of the original that may only be guessed at from those elements remaining the same in the various translations. This is somewhat like trying to pin the tail on the nonexistent donkey, but it is perhaps the best one can do with the limited resources of one language. Another method I have tried in order to gain a sense of tone and rhythm is to have someone who reads in the original language read the poem aloud to me several times. Then I try to carry the sense of that energy and tonality into my judgment of the poem translated into English.

One thing these amateur methods of judging the translation can't deliver is the loss of societal concepts which may not be carried intact from one language to another. I'm thinking of some things I learned about the nature of the old Irish language during my stay in Belfast. Irish speakers have no word for "no," for head-on refusal, and this has no doubt caused them to have to sit around drinking, telling stories, singing songs, having fun, and generally wasting their lives. (Even the advent of English has been unable to change this language-grown pattern.) The Irish speakers also have no word for "yes" and this causes all kinds of elaborate insecurities. Think of all those Irishmen waiting mournfully in pubs for their sweethearts to just "drop in" because there has been no way to be sure she'd turn up if they made a date. And her insulating herself with a crowd of women friends so she won't have to sit alone in the pub if he doesn't stop by.

When a language threatens to disappear through lack of usage, it threatens to take with it a whole range of emotions and attitudes. For instance, Irish is a language that has preserved a communal sense to the point that the idea of ownership doesn't exist. The idea of wife or husband or belonging or "mine" doesn't exist—only "she/he who is *with* me, who has come *along* with me."

So it is hard to tell whether or not the translator has gotten in touch with the cultural ideas and concepts of the country, its times and customs. If he hasn't, the translated poem may become a kind of awkward refugee in the new language, but only the culturally expert reader will know. The poem itself arrives as best it can, often having braved the flooded arroyo to stand dripping great embarrassing pools on the bourgeois carpet, impossibly wearing a sombrero.

When one considers that the craft of translating is at best approximate, and that American readers seldom know the language in which the poem originates, one wonders why we as readers and writers are so excited to be the purveyors and recipients of so much work in translation. After all, we do live with an entire country of writers who are working first and best in the language we were born to—English. Even Tomlinson speaks at the close of his introduction of the "inevitable but in some ways depressing translation boom of recent years."

Perhaps one of the first reasons for our attraction to poems in translation could be that we've been looking for spiritual qualities in foreign authors that often seem to be missing in our own contemporaries. I know that as a woman writer I had been unconsciously searching for a poet-heroine who was passionate, capable of supreme acts of the spirit; one who possessed intellect and personal dignity without disappearing over the horizon into the otherworldly. In my own poetic past

I had Emily Dickinson, who lived with her mother and fa-
ther—Emily with her reclusive long-distance battles with God
and a bodily death. I had Marianne Moore, who lived with
her mother and pirated from their conversations and also
those famed probings of the encyclopedia. In more recent
times there has been a spectrum of man-haters, sexual and
spiritual martyrs, suicides, placid say-no-evils, mild-mannered
girl reporters, and faithful red riding hoods—Plath and Sex-
ton, who courted their deaths, whether they intended it or not,
popularized taking one's life as the ultimate manifesto against
social and personal forces they no longer had the stamina to
argue with. It's no wonder that the Russian poet, Akhmatova,
in the translations by Stanley Kunitz, struck me as heroic, but at
the same time as more humanly approachable. Here was a
woman who could speak for a country and a time. A woman
who had the dignity of a witness, a survivor. Her son had been
imprisoned, her husband had been executed. She herself had
been haunted and spied upon, and forbidden to publish any-
thing for ten years. Her poems were sensual without being
indulgent. They carried the fullness of one who lived boldly
the risks of the spirit, the heart, and the body through a time
which could openly honor none of these. In short, someone to
aspire to. I know I'm not the only contemporary woman poet
deeply affected by these poems. Jane Kenyon has worked, with
the help of a Russian translator who knew Akhmatova, on a
book of Akhmatova's poems not translated elsewhere. It is
hard to quote the poems singly and give the sense of what
Kunitz accomplished in these translations, but here is a
sampling:

How can you look at the Neva,
how can you stand on the bridges? . . .
No wonder people think I grieve:
his image will not let me go.
Black angels' wings can cut one down,
I count the days till Judgment Day.
The streets are stained with lurid fires,
bonfires of roses in the snow.
("How Can You Look At The Neva")

Before these translations of Akhmatova appeared, Louise Bogan in *Blue Estuaries* had set the high mark for what I'd considered lyric poetic excellence. Bogan's poems seemed to have been hammered in bronze, the voice possessed of a reticence and wisdom. Yet at times I read her without comfort like the duped chimpanzee hugging the wire surrogate. Bogan's stony pride got in my way. I was yearning for a largeness of being that could be inclusive in its strengths, that took up the struggle without giving way to its most degrading aspects. In my heart of hearts I recognized Akhmatova. I had been on the waiting end of the Vietnam War, had lived with the spirit-death of my returned pilot-husband in whose silence the destroyed terrain with its ghosted villages and mountains reappeared. Until that meeting with Akhmatova in the Kunitz translations it had seemed impossible to speak with authority; and even as I finally wrote, addressing myself to her as in a letter meant to reach us both beyond our lives, I felt humbled, unequal to the events of her life.

Stepping Outside

for Akhmatova

Hearing of you, I never lost a brother
though I have, never saw a husband to war,
though I have, never kept with my father
the emptiness of his hands, my mother
the dying of her womb.

Return: husbands, sons, fathers return.
Many with both arms, with dreams
broken in both eyes.
They try, they try
but they cannot tell us
what comes back with them.

One more has planted his hoe
in my heart like an ax, my farmer uncle
slain by thieves
in the night, burned down
with his house, buried, dug up

to prove he was no dog.
He was no dog.

You, who lived in your pain until it grew
its own face, would have left all this
like a monument in a field. Your words
would have made a feast of what ate you.

Sit with me.
No one has left; no one returns.

The ambiguity of our own political, emotional, psychic, and spiritual energies has certainly played a part in our attraction to poems in translation. There are unspoken but obvious benefits for the poets who read in translation—that at the heart of some poets' voraciousness for translations are practical considerations like the need to steal from somebody who won't find you out, a kind of secret literary imperialism. After all, it hardly seems like stealing when it is already stamped with the approval of successive fingerprints. Also, the particular cozy use of the ego in American poetry in which the "I" seems often in exact coincidence with the poet in divulging the family secrets has produced in some poets a state of near-psychic bankruptcy. Frequent vacations to exotic lands have become a necessary and welcome relief.

The plunder we have brought back in the form of new subject matter from these excursions into the exotic lands of translations has perhaps been the most recognizable gain. That is, one could tell the prized remnant was intended to be a crocheted Brazilian hammock, but because it had to be thrown overboard to drag in one of the drunk passengers on the long ocean voyage over, it had shrunk incredibly and now resembled a pygmy slingshot.

I must admit that the whole panorama of literary adventure via translation has caused me to feel at times a mixture of amusement, excitement, and real curiosity about the reasons behind it. If my tone is somewhat ironic, it's because I'm drawn and repelled at the same time. Maybe it's the story of the woman with a spoon who meets the woman with a Mix-Master. Whatever it is, this abundance of poems in translation, we want it. It's new: it's different.

New Subject Matter

Where would we be without the voluptuous Spanish love of bones and death, the murders of passion, the particular irrational brand of surrealism that freed us from the calculated French version. What a relief whenever one slashed a wineskin to see your brother's blood "jump out," suddenly to have license to practice a kind of spastic surrealism. But also, for an American reader, there is the delight at finding a much-needed sense of humor in the Spanish attitude toward death as seen in "The Least Corpse" by Angel Gonzalez, translated by Robert Mezey. The poem, for an American reader, reverses the current dictum that one should live as long as possible no matter what state of decay and biological collapse the body undergoes. Here the friends of the corpse are anxious to get on with their mourning. "Die some more," they say. The corpse is in a state of embarrassment since he seems to retain several life signs (emotions, sneezing, coughing, talking), which make us feel that perhaps the dead may not be as removed from the living as we imagine.

When the corpse flicks the worm from its sleeve, then apologizes and puts it back on the sleeve, the invitation is both funny and pathetic. The corpse gives over his body to the worm's banquet, agrees to his transformation into feast. This agreement with one's death in its most corporeal sense seems alien to prevailing attitudes in America which urge life-extension as a matter of human rights regardless of the quality of that life once it has been extended. The corpse in the poem is an ironically familiar character to us in a time when medical technology is able to sustain the body's vital signs to the extent that the death-moment has now become ambiguous and hard to define.

> He had died only a few inches:
> a tiny death that had its effect
> on three rotten molars and one toenail
> on his so-called left foot and, surprise!
> a few hairs here and there.
> They mumbled the usual prayers:
> "O Lord, forgive those three molars

their iniquity, their sinful
chewing. Godless teeth,
but your own creatures, after all."
He was there himself,
solemn before
what there was of his mortal remains:
a filthy prosthesis and some hair.
Friends had come to comfort him
but they only deepened his sadness.
"This is impossible, it can't go on
this way. Or maybe we should say:
This ought to be speeded up.
Die some more. Die once and for all."
Dressed in mourning, he shook their hands
with that phony regret
you see at the worst funerals.
                              "I swear"
—overcome, he burst into tears—
"I want to extinguish my feelings,
I want to turn my life into stone,
my love into earth, my desire to ashes,
but I can't help it, I talk sometimes,
I move a bit, I even catch cold,
and naturally those who see me
deduce that I'm alive,
but it's not so:
you ought to know this, my friends,
even if I sneeze,
I'm a corpse, I couldn't be more dead."
Despondently he let fall his arms,
flicked a worm from his sleeve,
said, "Pardon me," and picked up the worm.
After all it was only a scrap
of all he was looking forward to.

Vital Subject Matter

The Russians with all those troikas that could possibly put
romance back into transportation. The Russians, looking at
the Neva, poems smuggled out in babushkas, severity, inter-
minable train rides through the Urals. The Russians. Snow,

snow, snow. Weariness. Inexpressible sadness. Partings. And of course, the prison camps.

There is an undeniable mythic credibility these writers attain through suffering, deprivation, and torture. American writers are responding to this. And why shouldn't they? American poets have had to be resourceful, going to a lot of trouble killing and punishing themselves, going crazy—all because poetry and being a poet does not have the same political status in a country which ignores what you say. Democracy is the worst possible condition for flamboyant, heroic gestures from a poet. If a poet writes a poem against General Motors—who cares? If a poet denounces nuclear power plants and Kentucky Fried Chicken or clearcut logging or supertankers or Bell Telephone—so what? No wonder Marianne Moore settled for defending the fast disappearing Musk Ox.

The worst that could happen to a poet in this country who found a worthy approach to a cause would be that he'd be published, not banned for years like Akhmatova or Mandelstam. The stories of the persecution of Russian poets became important during the early seventies in supplying a sense of consequence imaginatively to our own free status. Mendelstam's poems gained power with us through a combination of restraint and lyric necessity, and his poem "Tristia" in translations by Kunitz, W. S. Merwin and Clarence Brown, and David McDuff has become familiar to us all. Here in a translation of Mandelstam by McDuff is another small poem about the final moments before a couple must flee their home.

The poignancy of these last furtive moments of the "we" is expressed through the placement and naming of objects and through the hasty preparations they must make. The stillness in this poem is similar to that in Tomas Tranströmer's "4 A.M.: Track," a poem which has become a classic with many poets who read liberally in translation.

Perhaps it is the silence in this Mandelstam poem and in the Tranströmer poem which attracts American readers. A pianist I recently heard speak commented that music is really *made of silence*. He said that the quality of his audience's silence joins the piece of music as it is played. Poetry also communicates qualities of silence through the very sound it makes, even to the reader alone with the page. Reading Mandelstam in translation is an education in these silences. American poems often proceed with a headlong velocity, and we can learn much from the pacing of poems like the following:

> We shall sit together in the kitchen for a while.
> The white kerosene smells sweet.
>
> Sharp knife, a loaf of bread . . .
> If you like, burn the primus at full wick,
>
> and if not then gather string
> to tie the basket in before the dawn,
>
> so we can leave here for the station,
> Where we must hope no one will find us out.

Heroes and Subject Matter with Consequence

Lorca shot. Rafael Alberti in exile in Argentina with his "Sleep Walking Angels," his "Moldy Angels," his "Memories of Heaven." I was studying with Mark Strand at the time he was translating the Alberti poems and I remember vividly the excitement of being shown one of these from the book he was compiling, *The Owl's Insomnia*. It was entitled, unforgettably, "That Burning Horse in the Lost Forests." It used a relentless cataloguing of seemingly unrelated yet causal events which appealed to my own wish to somehow out-leap the reasoned linearity of most narrative structures. The poem also made use of a *predictive* voice that is rare in American contemporary verse. A passage will give some idea of the compelling intersections of fate with the incidental. The poem brings violently into view a sense of time which is at once stopped and ongoing.

> And that this was somebody buried with a silver watch in his
>   lower vest pocket,
> which meant that at one the islands would vanish,
> and at two the heads of the blackest bulls would turn white,

and at three a lead bullet would pierce the lonely host left
   out in the reliquary of a church lost at the crossing of
   two paths: one going to a whorehouse, the other to a
   health resort
   (and the watch on the dead man),
which meant that at four the swollen river carrying the
   skeleton of a fish hooked to the pantleg of a foreign
   sailor would flow past a reed,
and at five a toad lost among vegetables in a garden would
   be cut in two by the unexpected entry of a wheel from a
   cart capsized in a ditch,
and at six some unhappy cows would hurl themselves
   against the caboose of an express train,
and at seven some men on a street corner would stab a
   drunken girl stepping outside her door to throw
   clamshells and olive pits into the street
(and the watch on the dead man)

There is a coercion of happenings in the poem. The reader
is forced to apply meaning and connection to disparate events
by the insertion of the phrase "which meant," since it is used
as a verbal hinge between catalogues.

Another unusual quality of this poem is what I'll call its *X-
ray vision*. There is the sense that all matter is penetrable and
accessible to the mind, to the eye of the mind. In the poem we
receive events which are ordinarily withheld, either because
of the small scale of the happening (the toad sliced in two) or
by the unseen nature of the experience itself (the skeleton of
a fish in the river which is hooked to a sailor's pants leg). The
miraculous slips by as entirely possible in such a world, so that
we hardly blink when we're told of islands that vanish and
black bulls that turn white. In this way the miraculous does
more than coexist with "the real." The miraculous becomes
actual.

The Italians

Cesare Pavese, one of the poets in the mid-thirties who was
committed to the political left wing and imprisoned by the

fascist authorities when they discovered that workers were reading his poems. He had stopped writing about the old classical subjects and wrote instead about beggars, whores, and workers. He managed to outlive his exile and killed himself at forty-two in 1950. In the early seventies the poets I knew were searching the secondhand bookstores for his autobiography, *The Burning Brand*, which they tended to keep on their nightstands. In 1976 William Arrowsmith's translations, *Hard Labor*, came out in hardback only. It didn't matter. We had to afford it.

Perhaps our feeling for Pavese's poems has something to do with the recent cross-fertilization between prose and poetry in American writing. There is a prosaic flatness in Pavese that is attached, in my own mind, to a romantic vision pushed to its farthest extreme so that it denies its passion on one level while reinstating it by its very absence and restraint. The matter-of-factness of the speaker's attitude toward the death in this poem causes it to become a natural event, as remarkable and unremarkable as the little cloud that "no one even notices."

Prison: Poggio Reale

A small window on the sky
calms the heart; someone died here, at peace.
Outside are trees and clouds and earth
and sky. Up here only a whisper comes:
and blurred sounds of all of life.

The empty window
doesn't show the hills beneath the trees
and the river winding clearly in the distance.
The water is as clear as the breath of wind,
but nobody notices.

A cloud appears,
compact and white, and lingers in the square of sky.
It sees stunned hills and houses, everything
shining in the transparent air, sees lost birds
sailing in the sky. People pass quietly
along the river and no one even notices
the little cloud.

                    In the small window
the blue is empty now: into it falls the cry
of a bird, breaking the whisper. Maybe
that cloud is touching the tree or sinking into the river.
The man lying in the meadow ought to feel it
in the breathing of the grass. But he doesn't move his eyes,
only the grass moves. He must be dead.

Pavese is aware of negative space in a way that reminds us
continually that our view, like that of the prisoner, is partial—
as when "the empty window / doesn't show the hills beneath
the trees. . . ." There is also that silence which comes to us
when we feel the world's largeness and lack of need for us, as
in the imagining of our deaths, as when the man in the mead-
ow of this poem "ought" to feel the disappearance of the
cloud "in the breathing of the grass." But the man becomes
objectlike, resists motion, and this causes the grass which does
not move to seem more alive than the man. This poem re-
stores the perspective of man as a creature who, for all his
elaborate, yet limited understanding, must come to the fact of
his bodily disappearance, his eventual transparency in the
world.

More Hardships and Heroes

The Hungarians who started a revolution with poetry. The
Greek poet Yannis Ritsos. His father insane, his sisters insane.
For political reasons he was unable to publish for sixteen
years. He was imprisoned in 1948, endured physical and psy-
chological torture, spent four years in concentration camps.
Arrested again in 1967, a year and a half in prisons, exile
again. Perhaps it was his metaphorical extravagance that at-
tracted us, lines like "a shriek remains nailed in the dark
corridor like a big fishbone in the throat of an unknown
guest." A construction so extended and awkward that no
American writer could really get away with it.
    The Turkish poet, Nazim Hikmet, also came into our lives
with *Things I Didn't Know I Loved,* translated by Randy Blasing

and Mutlu Konuk. We wouldn't have known or cared whether these translations were bad. They touched us, these poems, many of them written from prison. His book came to our shelves and stayed there. We could feel the indomitability of the human spirit in these poems. We could feel the abundance of the world we had begun to take so for granted.

There is a spilling forth of love-energy in this poem: love for rain, for hills, for rivers, sparks flying from the engine of a train plunging through darkness. There is an exuberance in the tone, a sense of amazement that we are blessed with these natural miracles *all of the time,* yet are often blind to them much of our life. Not since Whitman have we heard in America a voice so freshly and convincingly reclaiming the world. In this passage from "Things I Didn't Know I Loved," Hikmet's prison life ironically returns him to a world of amplified richness:

> and here I've loved the river all this time
> whether motionless like this it curls skirting the hills
> European hills topped off with chateaus
> or whether it stretches out flat as far as the eye can see
> I know you can't wash in the same river even once
> I know the river will bring new lights that you will not see
> I know we live slightly longer than a horse and not nearly as
>   long as a crow
> I know this has troubled people before and will trouble
>   those after me
> I know all this has been said a thousand times before and
>   will be said after me
> . . . .
> moonlight the most false languid the most petitbourgeois
> strikes me
> I like it
> I didn't know I liked rain
> whether it falls like a fine net or splatters against the glass
> my heart leaves me tangled up in a net or trapped inside a drop
> and takes off for uncharted countries I didn't know I loved
> rain but why did I suddenly discover all these passions sitting
> by the window on the Prague-Berlin train
> is it because I lit my sixth cigarette

one alone is enough to kill me
is it because I'm almost dead from thinking about someone
    back in Moscow
her hair straw-blond eyelashes blue
the train plunges in through the pitch-black night
I never knew I liked the night pitch-black
sparks fly from the engine
I didn't know I loved sparks
I didn't know I loved so many things and I had to wait
    until I
was sixty to find it out sitting by the window on the Prague-
Berlin train watching the world disappear as if on a journey
from which one does not return

19 April 1962 Moscow

Another translation classic that we all shared was *An Anthology of Twentieth-Century Brazilian Poetry*, edited by Elizabeth Bishop. There are enough fine poems in this collection to suggest that we have hardly scratched the surface of all the good poetry being written by Brazilian poets. It was my first encounter with the poems of Carlos Drummond de Andrade. His poem, "Don't Kill Yourself," translated here by Elizabeth Bishop, is a caustic, unromantic exhortation to a heartsick lover:

Carlos, keep calm, love
is what you're seeing now:
today a kiss, tomorrow no kiss,
day after tomorrow's Sunday
and nobody knows what will happen
Monday.

It's useless to resist
or to commit suicide.
Don't kill yourself. Don't kill yourself!
Keep all of yourself for the nuptials
coming nobody knows when,
that is, if they ever come.

Love, Carlos, tellurian,
spent the night with you,
and now your insides are raising
an ineffable racket,

prayers,
victrolas,
saints crossing themselves,
ads for better soap,
a racket of which nobody
knows the why or wherefore.

In the meantime, you go on your way
vertical, melancholy.
You're the palm tree, you're the cry
nobody heard in the theatre
and all the lights went out.
Love in the dark, no love
in the daylight, is always sad,
sad, Carlos, my boy,
but tell it to nobody,
nobody knows nor shall know.

The private pain of the lover which is so often the very stuff of poems becomes in this poem a kind of false currency. We become aware of the lover's own aggrandizement of his pain, so much so that it hardly seems worth all that fuss. The oracular public voice in this poem is also an oddity to American readers who haven't heard anything approaching it since Auden in poems like "As I Walked Out One Evening."

Certainly the one thing we feel, reading all these translations from the Portuguese, is that several somebodies went to a lot of trouble inoculating those koala bears, getting passports, building elaborate cages, and shipping them all at great expense. It has to be worth it. And these must be the best, RARE in fact, the most cuddly, sociable ones to have been so chosen. Even if they eventually escape, they are of such good character and high breeding that they could only improve any ordinary brown bear they should happen to bump into.

Reading some translations, we get nostalgic for those early school days when everything was simpler. You moved from the Squirrels to the Bluebird reading group. That was progress—exchanging your bushy tail for wings. Dick and Jane fed Spot the eternal bone. A sentence had a subject, a verb, and an object, mostly in that order. The verbs were often transitive. "Spot chases the ball. The car hits Spot, Dick, and

Jane." There was a lot of listing and action. Roller-skating to the store to buy bread, eggs, peanut butter, and milk. Poetry in translation is sometimes like this, possessing a childlike freshness and simplicity. And because so many poets are reading in translation—as much as or more than they are reading poems of British or American origin—there has recently been the charge that translationese has begun to affect the diction, the rhythms, and the syntax of the English of contemporary poets, sometimes in an adverse way.

Reading poetry in translation has the deceptive effect of making you feel that anyone could write poetry and get away with it. There is a certain colorful abandonment in some translations that American poetry now wants to imitate.

Then too, we've gotten emotionally flat-footed in American poetry. All that restraint when we really wanted to belly-ache and be sentimental and effusive! We forgive the relative who arrives from the old country with all those quaint expressions, queer ways, but (and don't you forget it) "real character." We can talk soppily about the heart again, and tears and sorrows and pain. The spirit can sing, can soar, can be tender without apology, as in Vinicius de Moraes's "Song," translated by Richard Wilbur:

> Never take her away,
> The daughter whom you gave me,
> The gentle, moist, untroubled
> Small daughter whom you gave me;
> O let her heavenly babbling
> Beset me and enslave me.
> Don't take her; let her stay.
> Beset my heart, and win me,
> That I may put away
> The firstborn child within me,
> That cold, petrific, dry
> Daughter whom death once gave,
> Whose life is a long cry
> For milk she may not have,
> And who, in the night-time, calls me
> In the saddest voice that can be
> Father, Father, and tells me

Of the love she feels for me.
Don't let her go away,
Her whom you gave—my daughter—
Lest I should come to favor
That wilder one, that other
Who does not leave me ever.

I have not mentioned those other standbys of this rich time—Cavafy, Li-Po, Neruda, Lorca, Octavio Paz. Though we often can't tell how much fidelity the translations we read bear to their originals, we do know a good poem in English, and this seems to be the deciding factor in the translations that win us, although Linda Gregg made a good case *for* the awkwardness of poems in translation as a part of their authenticity when she spoke on translation with Galway Kinnell at the Roethke festival. Nonetheless, the fact that there are more good poets translating has meant that the quality of the poems in English has risen considerably, and this is a factor in drawing a large readership to these new voices entering our literature. If it's a mixed blessing, as it seems it is, the blessing is in our favor in the search for what is new and unforeseen. All the same, it is well to ask these questions as to the quality and use being made of this influx of poetry in translation. What do these poems provide that we've been missing? How, if at all, are they affecting the language and attitudes of our poems? In asking this last question we should remember the all-too-visible culprits in the erosion of English as it's written today—the communications media, the insistence on accessibility and literal clarity, the very pace at which we live.

Certainly one strong aspect of reading poetry in translation for one who does not speak or read other languages is the chance to enter the sense of a world literature as it tries on your language. It is the chance for a congregation of voices, and if it does not bring us into angel-hood, it will at least remind us of what we share with other poets in the way of subject matter and emotion, and more importantly, what our differences are. When poets go to poems in translation, they may not be altogether without ulterior motives, and this is perhaps because the poetic current Tomlinson asks for is alive in the best efforts of poet-translators. There is a vitality, as I've suggested, mainly of spirit; and it is a resource we are going to need more than any earthbound fuel. So if there is going to be imperialism, let it be literary and shamelessly beholding, a fading of the boundaries between *theirs* and *ours*, there in the poems where our words overlap and yes, imperfectly meet.

Again

*Some Thoughts on the Narrative Impulse in
Contemporary Poetry*

One has only to spend a day or two with a three-year-old to be reminded how deep and persistent the drive toward narrative, toward story, must be. When I served as children's librarian in Beaufort, South Carolina, during the Vietnam War, storytelling time was the only time I can honestly say my library was quiet. Children want to hear stories and they want to hear the same stories more than once. From my own childhood I can recall stories my father told which I listened to time and again—I truly craved, for instance, one about the time he and a friend nearly robbed the Seminole Bank in Seminole, Oklahoma. They plotted the act, drove the car to the bank, killed a bottle of whiskey between them, argued, fell asleep with a loaded gun in the car seat next to them, and woke up in the dark. I was still asking him to tell that story when he was seventy.

Recently my three-year-old niece, Rijl, spent a few days at my mother's house, and I felt as if I were watching some reincarnation of that energy with which I pursued stories as a child. All day Rijl patiently stalked readers. I became a veteran of *The Pokey Little Puppy* and *The Nursery Rhymes of Mother Goose*—this last a particularly treacherous piece of reading since she had memorized a good number of these poems and recited them like magical charms at accelerated speeds as I read—in effect, dispensing with me while her memory satisfied its own incantational needs.

It occurs to me, thinking of my own relationship to narrative, that the incantational is something I've associated more with lyrical poetry, when perhaps it is every bit as strong an element in the giving and hearing of stories. Certainly in reading or telling stories to children, one gets back in touch with that element in the fact that children are able to hear a story, then turn right around and hear it again. One also returns to a sense of the story as *treasure* in reading to children. That is, the excitement of the child in listening to stories reminds us that storytelling is discovery, is coming upon events as one might come upon buried treasure. This treasuring is also experienced in the way that a child reminds one that the story has boundaries, a fixed way it should be told; and one has only to stray from the telling in the slightest degree to encounter a child willing to shriek, cry, or pout in order to protect a particular version of the story. Perhaps this protection is a way of establishing the child's pleasure in what I'd like to call "again-ness."

During our family gathering I overheard my brother-in-law trying to break the rut of telling the same stories over and over to his daughter. He had decided to mix stories, and he led into it like this: "One day Goldilocks and Red Ridinghood met up in the park and put on their roller skates." "No! No! They didn't!" Rijl shouted. "But they were best friends," her father said, as if everyone should have known this. "No they weren't!" Rijl flung at him, and then as if to ward off this transgression, began repeating to herself in a kind of chant: "They weren't friends—they weren't friends—they weren't!"

It was not lack of imagination which led Rijl to reject her father's new use of these story characters, but rather her need to guarantee the "again-ness" of the story. How could she ever know what Goldilocks would be up to if she allowed her to get mixed up with Red Ridinghood? The idea of the Wolf might go astray, too. Anything could happen. The Wolf might eat both storybook girls and there would be no stories at all. Furthermore, she didn't like large amounts of contemporary life getting into her stories—those roller skates, for instance.

This resistance to modernity brings up something else that occurred to me about the impulse toward narrative in poems.

Perhaps in the case of storytelling, the poet must supplement Pound's dictum to "make it new" with an acknowledgment that the reader and listener may also need to "hear it old." This certainly goes back to storytelling's oral roots, in which mythmaking provided a tradition for scooping up history and fitting it to already existing mythical patterns. This allowed an injection of the new, while maintaining the fabric of the old. Through this process the heroes were gods at first, then kings and princes, then knights and soldiers, then gradually adventurers, religious crusaders, even robbers such as Robin Hood. Finally, we reach our present democratization of the poet-as-hero in which the poet's perception and deeds are themselves the engine of the narration. In those early times of the poet as singer, the speaker had no identity separate from the story s/he told. The poet was not an author, as we learn in a fascinating scholarly account of the beginnings of narrative poetry in *The Nature of Narrative* by Robert Scholes and Robert Kellogg.[1] That's why the names of the singers did not, as a matter of record, accompany the songs when they were eventually written down. These singers were performers, extraordinary performers, one must hasten to add, in that they were composing improvisationally, but they were not originators in the sense we usually mean when we use the terms "poet" and "author" nowadays.

So there has been an evolution in storytelling from singer and performer to author and the poet-as-hero. What was originally a more collaborative, improvisational process in the "making" of the narrative as in the time of *The Iliad* and *The Odyssey* (both composed orally), is, in contemporary poetry, as solitary an endeavor as the one we normally associate with the lyric sensibility in which the writer has traditionally expressed a more personal and even isolate vision.

Indeed it seems that the narrative and the lyric impulses in contemporary poetry have grown more and more indistinguishable. A clue to the reasons may be found in this shift from teller to maker. It is strange to remember in this time of poets as personalities that the singers of the narrative in its beginning did not attach their names to the songs like authors, although a singer might be associated with a particular song or referred to as "the one who carried it best." Some of the bardic rituals of song-giving still survive in Yugoslavia and in Ireland. Thinking about this matter of authorship reminded me of my recent experience of traditional Irish singing where it is a serious breach of etiquette for a singer *not* to precede the singing of a song with a simple statement of who it was that *gave* the singer that song. So in the Irish singing tradition, great respect is still accorded to the carrying-on of that tradition, and the singer is someone to whom there is as much reverence accorded as we feel for an originator of a story or poem.

This separation of the singer from the song happened when narrative ballads were published as broadsides and sold in the streets of London and elsewhere in the British Isles in the early sixteenth century. This broke with the courtesy of handing down songs by particular singers. Much later, in our own folk ballad tradition, there is the example of "The Ballad of Jesse James" to suggest that, as singers more and more assumed the status of writers, they wanted their names to stay with their songs. In this song the writer records his name in the penultimate verse, but he also speaks of himself in the third person, as if he were a character in the narrative:

> This song was made by Billy Gashade
> As soon as the news did arrive.
> He said there is no man with the law in his hand
> Can take Jesse James when alive.[2]

Even so, most of the printed versions have omitted this stanza.

This again-ness, made more conveniently available through the printing of narrative ballads, served to bring about the end of the oral tradition then, a tradition in which singers, as with contemporary lyric poets, were the ones who established the hear-it-old, the handing down of the song. Over a period of half a millenium this would result in anonymity for the singer and authorhood for the writer, and with this perhaps the diminution of an important secondary dimension of narrative—the sense of its having been treasured or "passed down." As writers of narrative gradually achieved the status of originators, they moved from the convention of an omniscient, anonymous teller to that of the current personal and intimate narrative of confidence-giving.

It is now the intimacy of voice, used as a poetic strategy, which establishes the hear-it-old requirement of the ancient narrative impulse—even though at first this intimacy might seem to accomplish exactly the opposite in making things feel all-too-much invested in the present moment. That is, hearing something told as-if-in-confidence establishes a context of "I'm only telling this to you." Giving a confidence implies exclusiveness, a one-time-only access. A sense of this "privileging" of what is told often accompanies the narrative as it is now carried by the personal "I" in the contemporary poetic narrative. But the ritual of confidence-giving and confidence-receiving is as old as speech itself. Consequently, as we hear this narrative as an *only,* we also hear it as an *always* since we feel the closure of confidence and intimacy which accompanies the telling. An entrustment, a treasuring, is being asked of us as receivers.

Since the poet has become the hero of the poem in the sense that the poetic *persona* and the poet's own autobiography are more closely engaged than at any other time in poetic history, we have what amounts to instant history and myth-making. Repugnant as this intimacy and egocentricity may be at times, it has enabled the poet to continue, in a sometimes too insistent yet often poignant way, to preserve the sense of value, of handed-downness, of treasuring what is told. The convention of intimacy, in this instance, serves as a kind of telescopic lens through which the poet's experience is actually magnified and brought emotionally close to the reader. It is as if this intimate speaker of contemporary poetic narratives has *always* known us and been able to speak frankly about the unspeakable with us. In this way, the tradition of hearing-it-old continues under different terms even as we hear it newly.

This intimate speaker in contemporary narrative is also responsible, perhaps, for the current phenomenon in which lyric poems seem to me to be almost entirely dependent on narrative, anecdotal strategies. This has greatly blurred the distinction between narrative and lyric. When one thinks of the "pure" lyric one thinks perhaps of poems like Yeats's "A Coat":

> I made my song a coat
> Covered with embroideries
> Out of old mythologies
> From heel to throat;
> But the fools caught it,
> Wore it in the world's eyes
> As though they'd wrought it.
> Song, let them take it,
> For there's more enterprise
> In walking naked.[3]

The poem is short, for one thing. Its energies affect us through metaphor more than through the rendering of a particular experience of coat wearing or coat thieving. It is invested more in song as an impassioned freeing of spirit than in either the giving of wisdom or the telling of *this* unrepeatable experience. The phrase "let them take it" is for me the emotional center of the poem. Just so, the "pure" lyric has been associated with the cry, the exclamation, the unanswerable voicing of states of being. Narratives, on the other hand, are devoted to rendering actual or imagined happenings in such a way that we are moved by our involvement with the characters to the point that we wholly enter the realm of story. Think, for instance, of *Don Juan,* or of Sir Walter Scott's *The Lady of the Lake,* or Coleridge's *Christabel* and *The Rime of the Ancient Mariner* for examples of the narrative poem at its vigorous best.

What we really have now in contemporary poetry is a hybrid of two forms, narrative and lyric. Just as we have the term "dramatic-narrative" to apply to a poem like Frost's "Death of the Hired Man," we now need a term like the "lyric-narrative" to describe the most prevalent contemporary development of these forms.

It is necessary to get one of these hybrids before us in order to explore other aspects of contemporary narrative poetry. Although the work of Bill Knott is so individual as to resist representing anything but itself, there is a poem in his new book, *Becos,* entitled "The Closet" in which the "emotional" narrative evolves through a combination of narratively linked images and scene giving. Both elements seem characteristic of the "lyric-narrative."

The "factual" narrative of "The Closet" is that of a child trying to witness his mother's death in childbirth and thereby free himself from the "secret" of her death. The poet-hero accomplishes this through constructing a series of images which allow him to reimagine the death. He also adopts a cinematic coldness toward the event itself so as to experience it more fully. Paradoxically, this process of removal, of "excluding" the self, allows the poet to address the child's inability to act. It is the story of the child conqueror and the paradigmatic myth of the breaking of a spell. The voice is that of an adult remembering this childhood experience, and the telling is, as with most lyric-narratives, an intimate one in which the autobiography of the poet's own mother's death is volunteered. In Knott's poem the child thinks of what the emptied closet felt like to the speaker as a child, of the emptied hangers as scalpels "glovelessly scraping uteri." The hangers are seen next as birds that by their wingspans "escape me" and then as "buzzards / measly as moths" over an "undotted desert" where the speaker seems as vulnerable as a rodent to forces which can "swoop sudden, crumple in secret"—as he has been crumpled emotionally on entering this closet. The narrative proceeds, then, through the transformation of the hanger image into other images. Eventually we turn to a scene in which the speaker imaginatively reenacts the grotesque operating room death of the mother in childbirth:

> . . . mobs of obstetrical
> Personnel kneel proudly, congratulatory, cooing
> And oohing and hold the dead infant up to the dead
> Woman's face as if for approval, the prompted
> Beholding, tears, a zoomshot kiss.[4]

By imaginatively witnessing the mock tableau the speaker seems able to marshal his attack not only against the mother's death, but against his own psychic death and loss of whole-ness. For the closet is a kind of coffin, we understand, when the speaker tells us it "has no windows." At the end of the poem, the poet returns to the "knife-'n'-slice" power of the hangers which he disarms by jumping up and "gropelessly" catching them in order to "twist them clear / Mis-shape them whole" as he is misshaping his mind whole in the narrative he tells himself in order to break the spell of his mother's disap-pearance into death. Knott ends the poem: "I shall find room enough here / By excluding myself; by excluding myself, I'll grow." So the end of the story is the poet-speaker's recogni-tion that birth is always the ultimate exclusion of the child by the mother, but that he can exclude himself—can create scenes in which he is not included so as to better see or imag-ine the meaning of events. The speaker has entered the womb of his own imagination which allows a kind of freedom within the small space of the closet-coffin. He regains the death of the mother in this way and repairs his original exclusion.

What qualifies this poem as a lyric-narrative for me is that it has both an interior (emotional progression) and an exterior (plot) narrative structure, along with the close proximity of the speaking voice to the identity of the poet himself—the poet is the hero, or rather, the poet's imagination is the hero. We "hear it old" in this narrative by virtue of the intimacy of the speaker's voice as it confides its fears and resolutions. The poet's voice here is in the same relation to the reader as it is to itself—that is, confessionally open.

As with Knott's poem, most narrative poems being written now seem to have an extremely vivid sense of scene which owes much to cinema, to the ability to "rack focus," to "zoom-shot" in on details the poet wants to amplify or distort. The seeing eye of the contemporary poet is progressively more cameralike in the giving of details—i.e., clinical, emotionally reserved. The narrative of the camera is one which often proceeds through juxtapositional cuts (à la *Potemkin*) rather than through expositional splicing, and this is especially adap-tive to poetry's ambition to move as quickly and compactly and intensely as possible through the narrative. Therefore, much of the pleasure of the lyric (which is fast-moving, compact, and emotionally intense) may now be accomplished as easily and perhaps even *more* easily in the narrative poem. I say "more easily" because there is always the sense in which any narrative poem propels a writer into the material so that the poem often seems to practically write itself once the poet begins to tell the story.

When the events of the poem are photographically rendered, the reader experiences them in a contemporary version of the "hear-it-old" oral narratives in that we feel camera-distanced, the scrapbook phenomenon of attending the fixed record of an event. At the same time, the scale of the event has been affected. The epic quality and larger-than-life scale we associate with films is present, has been superimposed upon the events of the poet's very life as they are presented to us. This reliance on cinematic devices may make less able writers feel that an experience is more implicit and available in narratives than it truly is.

This overaccreditation of "the real" is one of the reasons for so many boring narrative poems. What we get in bad narratives is the raw footage, or what they call in the movie business "the rushes." As with much amateur footage of the home-movie variety, the narrative poem is too often *camera-verité* at its worst: everything "larger than life" because it's shot in zooms or close-ups—long, intense pan-shots of the toddler crossing the dazzling vista of the backyard. The more the plots of poems have depended on "real life" happenings in the poet's own experience, the more myopic poets have become and, like the camera enthusiast, have mistakenly assumed that everything is, *of itself,* interesting. In cautioning my own writing students I have called this the "presentational mode."

While it is obvious that no basic narrative structure can be achieved without a certain valuing, subordination, and judging implicit in the process, it is even truer that bad poems result when the writer abdicates precisely these responsibilities. One of the main faults I encounter with students who attempt to write narrative poems is that they become so "presentational" that they not only let go of the steering wheel, they leap like Hollywood stunt men from the moving vehicle and allow it to crash, spectacularly unattended, into the gorge. They don't accept the responsibility for directing the narrative or making it bear consequence in our lives.

When we study the plots in the old lyrical folk ballads we learned as children, it becomes clear that a fatedness, a quality of inevitability, was there to instill a feeling of consequence. This is true in both "The Ballad of Jesse James" and "Sir Patrick Spence." As in the best narratives, the writers knew what to leave out and how to gain our respect and sympathy for their heroes. One of the things I love about "Sir Patrick Spence" is that we're never told the most crucial element of the narrative—that Sir Patrick's ship sinks. Rather, we infer this delightedly, since we're given only the foreboding:

> O lang, lang may their ladies sit,
> Wi thair fans into their hand
> Or eir they se Sir Patrick Spence
> Cum sailing to the land.

Then we see the ladies "Wi their gold kems in their hair / Waiting for thar ain deir lords / For they'll see thame na mair." And in the last lines:

> Haf Owre, haf owre to Aberdour,
> It's fiftie fadom deip,
> And thair lies guid Sir Patrick Spence.
> Wi the Scots lord at his feit.

In the early verses of the ballad, suspense is built up through the fact that Sir Patrick has no choice when asked by his king to sail this ship, even though it is a treacherous time of the year. We hear his reluctance along with the premonitions of his men:

> "Late, late yestreen I saw the new moone,
> Wi the auld moone in her arme,
> And I feir, I feir, my deir master,
> That we will cum to harme."[5]

Lacking the repetition, rhymes, and refrains which the ballad carries as its tradition, the free verse narrative has a harder time discovering strategies with which to give itself musical consequence. This causes it to depend on voice to a much greater extent than did the anonymous, omniscient narratives of the past.

One of the best contemporary writers of the free verse narrative poem, Louis Simpson, points out in his essay, "Irregular Impulses: Some Remarks on Free Verse,"[6] that narratives in free verse had better be short. The reason he gives is that regular verse could go on for some time without doing or saying anything remarkable because one had at least the pleasure of the regularity, the musical quality. But the irregularities of free verse, Simpson suggests, necessitate content, something to say, and an interesting, compelling way to say it. If the free verse narrative is going to be shorter, it means that the narrative poem is going to look more and more like the lyric and less and less like the epic mammoths of Ermoldus Nigellus, which ran to twenty-five hundred lines of elegiac couplets, or the verse annals of Charlemagne, which reach nearly three thousand hexameters and elegiac couplets. Simpson singles out Patrick Kavanagh's *The Great Hunger* as a poem in free verse which runs to over eight hundred lines yet manages to sustain interest. It does so, Simpson says, because it has a theme, which he contends "most American poets lack."

It seems to me that there is a problem in discussing narrative once we are asked to separate "theme" as a concept from other attributes of the narrative. Implicit in any act of narration is the assumption that whatever is to be understood or passed on can only be given exactly in the way in which it has been given. Nonetheless, Simpson's formal and artificial separation of theme from story does allow one to conjecture as to the reasons for the writing of so many narrative poems of late. Perhaps "story" itself is now replacing "theme" as poets attempt to show how they arrive at what they value in their experience. One attribute of storytelling is its reluctance to summarize event into meaning, to reduce content to moral or even to statement—in other words, a rejection to some extent of the poet's control over and commentary upon the events of the narrative.

The description and history of narrative poetry given in the *Princeton Encyclopedia of Poetry* reads like an obituary for the narrative poem which, according to the text, has been replaced by the lyric or the "fashionably dramatic."[7] Our own age is reported to have "scorned narrative poetry in general and sought its stories for entertainment, instruction, or artistic edification in the novel." Well, it ain't so. Just as the short story has surges in popularity and recognition and then develops quietly for a period before a new emergence, the narrative poem has always been there waiting to reassert itself. With the free verse narrative poem's annexation of lyric strategies, it has become once again a creditable and innovative arena for many of our best poets to try their skills. One need only open any "little magazine" to experience the garden variety of lyric-narrative poem, so to name its practitioners would not further this discussion. The narratives which stand out in my memory from the generation of poets immediately ahead of me give indications of diversity and stamina for what one might call the *longer* lyric-narrative poem—that which points toward epic ambitions, but without the length or really the adherence to story which epic implies. I'm thinking here of Hayden Carruth's *The Sleeping Beauty*, and of his more colloquial poems written in the voices of Vermont natives. Carolyn Kizer has a long narrative on the life of Mrs. Stevenson and another entitled "Fanny," about her meeting as a young girl with Einstein—both admirable for their skill with narrative. Stanley Kunitz's poem on Lincoln and his "The Wellfleet Whale" are also fine narratives. Another favorite of mine is Donald Hall's "Names of Horses," from *Kicking the Leaves*. The entire *Book of Nightmares* by Galway Kinnell ought to be mentioned, along with his great poem, "The Bear," as establishing and widening our sense of what is possible in combining the lyric with the narrative impulse. There are poems—James Wright's "At the Convicted Murderer's Grave" and Robert Lowell's "Terminal Days at Beverly Farms," to name just two—which remain examples for me of how well the lyric-narrative carries story past the facts of the case into contradictions which test our minds and spirits, and point toward the life choices we are making and watching others make.

Among my contemporaries, those successfully writing the lyric-narrative would have to include Stephen Dobyns (*Black Dog, Red Dog*), Charles Wright (*The Other Side of the River*), Robert Hass (*Praise*), Linda Gregg's longer poems in *Too Bright to See,* Mary Oliver's more historical poems in *American Primitive*, C. K. Williams (*Tar*), Robert Pinsky (*History of My Heart*), Gerald Stern (*Lucky Life*), and effectively more writers than I can properly think to name here. Jack Gilbert's *Monolithos* seems to me to be holding down the fort for the lyric. For one thing, he's using a shorter line than the others I've named and is still trying to condense rather than expand the form. Carolyn Forché is working more out of the dramatic-narrative tradition, although her use of El Salvador in *The Country Between Us* depends so heavily on voice and a content which would be journalistic if not for her way of mythologizing it through rhetorical strategies, that I tend to think of her as a writer who crosses categories. Still, it is the narrative which carries the burden of content in her poems too.

It is exactly the way in which free verse narrative necessitates attention to "content" (what is happening, to whom, and why it matters) which has begun to free the best contemporary poetry from much of the listless autobiography begun in the sixties and seventies. There seems now to be an evolving sense of others and otherness in poems, an exodus out of the cramped "I." One of the things narrative tends to do in poems is to enlarge the cast and the setting. If ever such an enlargement were needed, it is here in good old Ayn Rand, me-first America.

I recently met James Dickey at a reading he gave in Baton Rouge, Louisiana. It was one of those evenings in which you realize you are in the presence of a born storyteller who is performing for an audience of born story-listeners. When both are present, the occasion has magnitude. He read "The Sheep Child" which I had all but forgotten, and it astounded me anew, both for its rescue of the outrageous in its content and for the spell of the story itself. What I'm coming to is what this consummate storyteller said to me after the reading—the gist of which was, that he was tired of the anecdotal in his own poems. I assume he was referring to the story as that creature of itself which invites and rewards by its very reluctance to do anything but be told. I gathered that he was tired of using story to carry content in this way. What then did he propose in its place? I asked. He wanted the oracular. The poet speaking in the riddles of the oracle. Not narrative but divination. The water-witcher, not the farmer. It occurred to me that what Dickey may have been missing in narrative poetry was the kind of mystery and mystification that the oracular insists on posing for the reader *and* the writer. I have already written an essay on the oracular mode as it relates to the poetry of Michael Burkard,[8] so I won't examine this further here, except to note Dickey's defection to the oracular as perhaps suggesting that for Dickey at this point, narrative no longer satisfies his need for mystery in the process of his writing.

As much as I admire many dimensions of the oracular poem, this mode in relation to the narrative seems to substitute one reluctance for another. If one of the main weaknesses of narrative is that it often seems to allow a poet to evade responsibility for his own attitudes toward the subject matter (i.e., to stand as mere witness), the oracular voice allows the poet not to know what is being received and then transmitted. This latter has its pleasures and is indeed part of any kind of imaginative writing—that we work out of our own unknowing. But at a time when nuclear annihilation is the pervading fear, it is hard to feel that the oracular is anything but a retreat, though its resources are as old and as central to poetry as are those of the narrative.

Because of our attraction to realism and simple human interest, lyric-narrative poetry has recently become the most popular form and at the same time a form somewhat despised for its easy accessibility, whose association with the word "linear" would ask us to believe that the narrative poet needs no finesse, no savvy, and takes no innovative gambles. Not so.

For one thing, the best narratives are masterful in their use of juxtaposition in order to move backward and forward in time and also in their use of statement, image, and scene. Even to begin to talk about the innovations that have come about through narrative poetry's approach to its proper subjects would demand an entire essay in itself. What I have done here is simply some map-making to put a new term, lyric-narrative, before us and to help locate its development within the tradition of narrative.

It is, finally, the form I most want to say "again" to in my own work. In writing the narrative, I'm much less sure when I'm in poem-territory than I am with the fast-disappearing lyric. And this is exactly the excitement. While it is true that recent narrative poetry has made me feel that poetry depends less on diction and image and metaphor than it does on voice and content, these elements of the lyric are still the resources of what I've been calling here the lyric-narrative.

In my own work, I keep trying to find ways to tell stories that have a largesse of spirit and reflect the dilemmas of those whose stories would never be told if I weren't there to witness and give voice. My early love of the ballad makes me want to infuse the prosaic quality of narrative with a lyric intensity at points, like the studs the carpenter puts in to hold up the weight of the house. In the end, the challenge with narrative or lyric or, for that matter, oracular poetry is the same—whether or not the reader is going to feel compelled to read those poems again and again.

NOTES

1. Robert Scholes and Robert Kellogg, *The Nature of Narrative* (New York: Oxford University Press, 1966).

2. *American Folk Poetry,* ed. Duncan Emrich (Boston: Little, Brown, 1974).

3. W. B. Yeats, *The Collected Poems of W. B. Yeats* (New York: Macmillan, 1963), 125.

4. Bill Knott, *Becos* (New York: Random House, 1983).

5. All verses are from Cleanth Brooks and Robert Penn Warren, *Understanding Poetry,* 4th ed. (New York: Holt, Rinehart, 1976).

6. *Ohio Review,* no. 28 (1982).

7. *The Princeton Encyclopedia of Poetry,* ed. Alex Preminger (Princeton: Princeton University Press, 1972), 550.

8. Tess Gallagher, "Inside the Kaleidoscope: The Poetry of Michael Burkard," *American Poetry Review* 11, no. 3 (1982): 34–41. Reprinted in this collection.

Sing It Rough

There are aspects of the writer-reader relationship which sometimes drive a poet to apology and denial. Readers, of course, are more likely to put their faith in a piece of writing when they feel there's a reasonable explanation for the choices the writer is making. They want order and magic at once. But the magic of poetry so often works against the taxidermy of logic and the reasoned apprehension of experience, that the poet turns outlaw when the reader wants to bulldog a poem into one-two-three-four meaning.

One of the stories I've found myself telling to explain the mystery out of the title, "Each Bird Walking," does, I think, have a good deal to do with the interiors of the poem. When I was a child I used to chase pigeons while my mother paused to chat with friends she encountered on our shopping trips into town. I wanted desperately to catch a pigeon, just one, to see what a pigeon felt like. My mother would buy some fresh popcorn from the dime store and I would tempt the pigeons round and round the parking meters until clouds of birds had carried off the last puff and kernel I had to offer. Although I was never once successful, I kept thinking that, finally, with the right agility and stealth, I would eventually lay hands on a pigeon. I assumed from the start that birds must be of a higher order than people. Birds could fly over entire towns and forests. The gulls of this seaport could not only fly, but could alight on water or fly up into the hemlocks. Why shouldn't I think birds were miracles? But there was also this curious two-footed walking around they did. As I flung out my popcorn week after week, I puzzled on this: why, if they could fly, did birds bother to come down at all and walk around the ankles of shopkeepers and children?

Then, in my perverse way, I began to think it wasn't so much the birds' flying that was exceptional, but this arduous walking, this dodging and skittering, this strutting and hop-flying, peck-walking they did among humans. Why humble themselves so if they could soar like angels?

In telling this story I manage to reawaken a sense of humor and an awareness of the miraculous in the readers who need reasons. They seem to remember what it is to have been a child and to have wanted to catch birds. Then I speak about the way in which birds have been identified as emblematic of the spirit in scriptural texts. Birds, according to Jungian chartings of the archetypal unconscious, have represented the spirit in countless ancient and not-so-ancient cultures. I remind my listeners, many of whom have not the slightest interest in either birds or the archetypal unconscious, that birds have often been represented as the message bearers of gods. When a spirit leaves a body, I add, it was sometimes seen to do so in the shape of a bird, often a dove. I feel myself getting perilously close to "the point." And, of course, the closer I get to making it—the point—the more I want to tell yet another story about birds and childhood. Then, before I can stop myself, I have said: "Sometimes the spirit, like a bird, has to walk, has to humble itself and do the unassuming, ordinary, necessary, the daily thing in order to attend most to its life and the lives of others." "Each Bird Walking" is a title that doesn't explain, but *illuminates* the poem in the way a kite tells us the currents of wind by its swoops and feints toward earth.

"But there are no birds in your poem."

I have to hear this remark. The speaker has cupped her hands into a megaphone and is standing like a karate expert, feet wide apart in the aisle. No, there are no birds in my poem. There is a son, a mother, and a speaker. They are each doing the painful but matter-of-fact caretaking that must be done, and this doesn't look miraculous, though it is. The son is walking, is calmly going about the step-by-step motions of attending a life on its way to death. The speaker walks in the sense of knowing that this love must end, yet must be carried into memory with dignity and meaning. In the title, the mention of birds walking reads like the attraction of place-names called out on a train in a foreign country, countries that will remain foreign. You can't get off the train to investigate, but an aura of excitement surrounds each of the names. You know they are the right and only names to designate exactly those places. You don't know why, but you know.

Each Bird Walking

Not while, but long after he had told me,
I thought of him, washing his mother, his
bending over the bed and taking back
the covers. There was a basin of water
and he dipped a washrag in and
out of the basin, the rag
dripping a little onto the sheet as he
turned from the bedside to the nightstand
and back, there being no place

on her body he shouldn't touch because
he had to and she helped him, moving
the little she could, lifting so he could
wipe under her arms, a dipping motion
in the hollow. Then working up from
the feet, around the ankles, over the
knees. And this last, opening
her thighs and running the rag firmly
and with the cleaning thought
up through her crotch, between the lips,
over the V of thin hairs—

as though he were a mother
who had the excuse of cleaning to touch
with love and indifference,
the secret parts of her child, to graze
the sleepy sexlessness in its waiting
to find out what to do for the sake
of the body, for the sake of what only
the body can do for itself.

So his hand, softly at the place
of his birth-light. And she, eyes deepened
and closed in the dim room.
And because he told me her death as
important to his being with her,
I could love him another way. Not
of the body alone, or of its making,
but carried in the white spires of trembling
until what spirit, what breath we were
was shaken from us. Small then,
the word *holy*.

He turned her on her stomach
and washed the blades of her shoulders, the
small of the back. "That's good," she said,
"that's enough."
On our lips that morning, the tart juice
of the mothers, so strong in remembrance, no
asking, no giving, and what you said, this
being the end of our loving, so as not to hurt
the closer one to you, made me look
to see what was left of us
with our sex taken away. "Tell me," I said,
"something I can't forget." Then the story of
your mother, and when you finished
I said, "That's good, that's enough."

One of the things this poem generates, besides questions
for which there are no satisfactory answers, is a need for
storytelling. I have been amazed at how many men from au-
diences have come up to me after hearing the poem and have
told how they've nursed their fathers, wives, or brothers
through final days and nights. There is something composed
and humble about these men who feel invited by the poem to
share with me. Their tenderness shines forth. The world is
richer.

When a taboo is broken there is often the feeling of fresh-
ness, a freeing of breath as it rushes in. Because I tell this
story of a son and his mother, I break the ancient taboo
against touching between mother and son. Throughout the
course of civilization women have been the caretakers of the

body during birth, illness, and death. The poem, by showing a man in this role, enlarges the share men may have in this experience.

There is nothing technically exceptional about the poem. Its poetry, in a very specific sense, resides partly in its challenge of the convention that sons may not intimately approach the bodies of their mothers after puberty. In a more general sense, it is the conception and presentation of a new arena of feeling and being which makes for poetry, a poetry concerned with forms of value in our lives. The gift of this poem, then, is the communal lifting of barriers to love—even if only for this deathbed ritual where it can hardly be refused. Also, by showing this son ministering to the mother, the poem returns positive energy to the mother-son relationship, which has most often been represented as claustrophobic and deserving of much agility on the part of sons in order to remain dutiful but distant, affectionate instead of loving, kind but certainly never devoted.

The speaker, the "I" of the poem, stays purposefully in the background. I say purposefully because the speaker is most valuable as witness here. Perhaps this humility of approach carries the reserve of emotion we know the speaker obeys in the last words of the poem: "That's good, that's enough." The ending places value in the idea of knowing when the good has come to its fruition, of accepting its end as fulfillment and not as deprivation or injury. This withholding of the "I" allows the reader a larger participation in the acts of the poem. The description of the washing is done in such a way that the goodness and beauty of the act happen as if to the reader as well as to the mother. The reader imaginatively associates with the body of the mother and is cleansed by the words of the poem. The reader also becomes the speaker of the poem, who must give over the intimacy of touch for the intimacy of telling. Perhaps there is illumination, too, in the reversal of roles: the son as mother, returning the care he's received as an infant; the mother completing her life in the needfulness she began with, the needfulness with which each of us begins.

Although the poem is scrupulously nonsexual in its language and intent, it is, for me in the telling, an extremely sensual poem, a poem which caresses and honors the body. The senses are at once stimulated by the recognition of the taboo at the unconscious level, yet normalized by the explicit, sacramental detailing and pacing of the poem. At the close of the poem, we are carried beyond the physical as the story opens into the ongoing memory of the speaker and consequently enters the memory of the reader.

Because I have disappeared into "story" in the writing of the poem, the language also disappears, does not call attention to itself. Its exactness comes from the authenticity of its tone, its empathy with its characters and their acts, and the urgency of felt knowledge working at an intuitive level to make this occasion unforgettable. As Wendell Berry has said, "Things that mattered to me once / won't matter any more, / for I have left the safe shore where magnificence of art / could suffice my heart." For me, this does not mean that one does not choose the right words or forgets that a poem is also music. It means there are always things at stake in the poem that make demands which artifice alone cannot deliver. As a singer and Irish musician friend of mine, Cahíl McConnel, says:

> You can sing sweet
> and get the song sung
> but to get to the third
> dimension you have to sing it
> rough, hurt the tune a little. Put
> enough strength to it
> that the notes slip. Then
> something else happens. The song
> gets large.

This hurting of the tune is crucial for my growth as a writer now, for I've known all along how to "sing sweet." Certainly there are legions who're singing sweet, hitting all the expected notes at the right intervals. But how to hit the wrong notes because that's where the feeling takes you and because you have to go there or lose your life—the meaningfulness and intensity of this kind of struggle in the writing can't be carried by artifice. Call it heart. Call it gift and passion and courage of the sort that causes the poet's voice to inspire the reader with belief in the real and marvelous at once. Like that point which long-distance runners describe where the legs disappear, where the consciousness of legs dissolves, the spirit infuses language to the degree that it does not exist as separate from the activity—the telling, the singing, the giving over of the "I" to an energy *of* the self, yet beyond it.

The movement of the poem "Each Bird Walking" is toward a conjunction of partings: mother from son, son from mother, and lover from lover. The human miracle of the poem is that, unlike so many partings, this one did not end in damage and forgetting. Life attitude is as much and likely more a part of what makes for largesse in poetry than diction, voice, tone, or strategy. If I can't respect the motives and meanings of a poem—the values at work there—it matters little what pyrotechnics, what calisthenics of metaphor, of imagery or rhythm the writer displays.

"There's a live one," the poet Guillevic said to his interpreter as he shook the hand of someone he was meeting at a book signing in Killarney. He knew the current was on. The hand belonged to the living. It squeezed into his in such a way that the meeting took place. "Don't ghost it. Sing it rough," I tell myself heading into a poem. I want the meetings to take place, even after the book is closed and the poem is a thing remembered.

The Poem as Time Machine

Once, at an auction in upstate New York, I watched two men carry a mahogany box with a crank handle onto the lawn. One of the men turned the lever until he was satisfied and then put a large black disk into the box and opened the front of the box so the little doors, spread wide, made the whole contraption seem as though it might fly away. But instead, a chorus of voices, recorded many years before, scratched and muted by all that intervening time and space, drifted out over the crowd.

Before anyone in our group knew what I was doing, I had signaled my way to ownership and the two men were approaching us carrying the Victrola, its record still turning above their heads.

In hearing the phonograph I had not forgotten life in the jet age; in fact, the simultaneity of jets and hand-wound phonographs had only amplified my amazement with both inventions. A few months before, I had been in Iowa; then in hours I was in New York. The morning of the auction I had spoken by telephone with my parents on the West Coast. That night I would watch a TV news reporter in Egypt, another in Israel. Still, all these inventions for transcending time and distance had not kept me from the original magic of the phonograph music. I did not exclaim: "See how they used to do it," but rather: "Voices out of a flat disk, human voices singing out of a mahogany box!" I was like an astronaut dropped suddenly into my own moment.

I remember the day my father came home from the neighbors' in 1949 and said they had a radio with talking pictures. It was his way of explaining television to us in terms of what he knew: radio. Several years later I would sit on the rug with half a dozen neighborhood kids at the house down the block, watching Flash Gordon and advertisements for Buster Brown shoes.

Such early space-travel films may have marked my first encounter with the idea of time machines, those phone booths with the capacity to transport one into encounters with Napoleon or to propel one ahead into dilemmas on distant planets. I was six or seven years old and already leading a double life as an imagined horse disguised as a young girl. I had long brown hair and a young friend named Koene Rasanen who suffered from the same delusions, which were, oddly, tolerated by our parents. There were several ridges behind my house which our horse-selves delighted in. Some of my freest moments still exist in those images of myself standing silhouetted on the highest knoll, pawing with one foot, tossing my thick pony mane and neighing for my friend with such authority that a real horse pastured down the block began to answer me.

To be called to the house to run errands or peel potatoes for dinner was to suffer a temporary malfunction of the time machine. Adults were those creatures who had suffered permanent malfunctions. If you neighed at them, they put it down to a sexual phase, or took it as a practical cue to shop for a horse.

When I got my first horse, at age ten, it was strangely unsatisfying. Already that exchange of the real object for the imagined embodiment had begun to disinherit me. I hadn't wanted a horse to ride, I had wanted to *be* a horse, and had, in the nearest human proximity, managed it.

Flash Gordon never became a horse by stepping into a time machine, but he could choose any one of countless masquerades at crucial moments in history or in the futures he hoped to outsmart. The whole idea of past or future being accessible at the push of a button seemed so natural to me as a child that I have been waiting for science to catch up to the idea ever since.

In the meantime, there have been a few wonderful gimmicks—Polaroid cameras and even Polaroid movie cameras:

instruments built to surprise the moment by reproducing it as close to its occurrence as possible, thereby extending the past-as-present, a spectator's present at that. So we have Mother tying the bow in Polly's hair. And if we like, we can run the film backward and untie Polly's hair. We have then an on-going past as a spectator's present.

With the country in a state of constant mobility, we depend more than ever on telephones to keep friends who have been left behind at the last outpost. We can be in immediate touch. Two disparate people living in the "now" may hook up across the miles, talking their pasts into the present up to that point where the pie is burning in the oven or where someone has knocked at the door. We may hurtle the body through space into exotic places on jets. It costs a lot *not* to be where you're expected to be . . . that trip you took to get away from the familiar faces, those phone calls you charged to make up for having forgotten those people who are truly living too far away to be held constantly in mind. Already we are shaking ghosts like shaking hands, meeting ourselves as has-beens where we stand.

I can still see Mark Strand shuffling the poems on his knees in a classroom in Seattle, Washington, in 1970 and saying in that ironic, ghost-ship voice of his: "Time, that's the *only* problem."

Octavio Paz defined the poet's time as "living for each day; and living it, simultaneously, in two contradictory ways: as if it were endless and as if it would end right now." Stanley Kunitz has written a poem entitled "Change," which gives this dual sense of impermanence and the desire to be eternal. He also includes memory as it comments upon the present moment, often painfully.

> Dissolving in the chemic vat
> Of time, man (gristle and fat),
> Corrupting on a rock in space
> That crumbles, lifts his impermanent face
> To watch the stars, his brain locked tight
> Against the tall revolving night.
> Yet is he neither here nor there

Because the mind moves everywhere;
And he is neither now or then
Because tomorrow comes again
Foreshadowed, and the ragged wing
Of yesterday's remembering
Cuts sharply the immediate moon;
Nor is he always: late and soon
Becoming, never being, till
Becoming is a being still.

Here, Now, and Always, man would be
Inviolate eternally:
This is his spirit's trinity.

Always, as a maker of poems, I have been witness to the images, have been led by the poem as it speaks into and with itself and opens out of its contradictions to engage the reader. But the reader is also the maker of the poem as it lives again in his consciousness, his needs, his reception, and even his denials. The poem is in a state of perpetual formation and disintegration. It is not at the mercy of pure subjectivity, but, as Ortega y Gasset would say, it is "the intersection of the different points of view." This, then, brings about a succession of interpretations of which no single one, even that of the poet, is the definitive one. In this way the poem enters and *becomes* time. It becomes, as Paz phrases it, "the space that is energy itself, not a container but an engenderer, a catalytic arena open on all sides to the past, on all sides to the future."

This conception of time as an atmosphere, as the "now" of the poem, which Paz calls "the Historical Now" or "the Archetypal Now," is what I would like to call "the point of all possibilities." By this I mean the point at which anything that has happened to me, or any past that I can encourage to enrich my own vision, is allowed to intersect with a present moment, as in a creation, as in a poem. And its regrets or expectations or promises or failures or any supposition I can bring to it may give significance to this moment which is the language moving in and out of my life and my life as it meets and enters the lives of others.

"Poems," says Paz, "search for the you." In America we begin to ask who will colonize the "I," that island of cannibals,

93

of separations, of endings and be-alls, of my-turn, of better-than-you, of privilege and sweat-of-the-brow rectitude, of I own this and you own that, homeland of the civilized heart-break where, if you leave, I shall get along anyway, I shall do perfectly well without you. There are others and others and you will not be one of them, where if your coat were drowning, I would not save it. No, the "I" without its search for the "you"—either by implication as the "I" in each of us or in a direct reaching toward the other—this "I," whose reaching *in* is not at the same time a reaching *out*, is like a character in a novel who is running on empty. We cannot long be interested in its roadside reveries, its monologues with the vast interiors. Even if you are speaking to a "you" that will not listen, it is better than no "you" at all. This includes the "you" that is the self, of course, but as "other." We remember Yeats speaking endlessly to Maud Gonne; Emily Dickinson talking to Death as if to a suitor; Hamlet confiding in a skull; Colette, who, when her mother died, saw no reason to stop writing letters to her.

The time of the "I" is expanded when it considers the "you," and perhaps the time the poem makes allows us to find courage for the risks yet to be taken in our "walking-around" lives. The poem not only makes time, it *is* time; it is made of time as is the bee who dances out the directions that are and are not the map of a place, but the remembering of a way back to the flower feast that belongs to others, to the hive, and to the very moment in which that way is given.

I have, in a poem, called a man back from the dead if he has not answered me fully in life. Yeats, in "He Wishes His Beloved Were Dead," even rushes ahead of a death to gain the right urgency in which he might be granted forgiveness.

> Were you but lying cold and dead,
> And lights were paling out of the West,
> You would come hither, and bend your head,
> And I would lay my head on your breast;
> And you would murmur tender words,
> Forgiving me, because you were dead:
> Nor would you rise and hasten away,
> Though you have the will of the wild birds,

But know your hair was bound and wound
About the stars and moon and sun.

The time of the poem is not linear, is not the time of "this happened, then this, then this," though I may speak in that way until I am followed and the language leads me out of its use into its possibilities. No one is buried so deeply in the past that he may not enter the moment of the poem, the point of all possibilities where the words give breath, in a reimagining. If the language of commerce is a parade, then the language of the poem is that of a hive where one may be stung into recognition by words that have the power to create images strong enough to change our own lives as we imagine and live them. The poet between poems is like a child called into the house to peel potatoes for supper. The time of the house is enigma to him. He cannot wait to be out the door again. *Time Is a River without Banks* is the title of Chagall's painting of the winged fish flying through the air above the river. The fish is playing a fiddle above a clock which flies with it. In order to indicate the river there are houses and lovers and the reflections of houses. The lovers are not looking up. They are in love and at the point of all possibilities. They have transcended time, which is all around them like the unheard music of the fiddle.

It is the poet who refuses to believe in time as a container, who rushes into the closed room of time, who plunges through the bay window and slashes a hand across the harp, even if what results is not music so much as a passionate desecration of a moment, which, like the photograph in its effort to fix us, excludes us from our own past. The poet is always the enemy of the photograph. If she talks about her own appearance in the group smiling on the porch, she will inch her thumb into the lens to indicate that she has escaped. She will assault the image with words, changing the bride's dress into a cascade of petals. She will make sure the train pulls away from the platform.

The poem as time machine works in an opposite way from the time machine as used in H. G. Wells. In the latter, one is sent out like a lonely projectile into time past or future, casting the present into a future or a past. The poem, on the other hand, is like a magnet which draws into it events and beings from all possible past, present, and future contexts of the speaker. It is a vortex of associative phenomena. "A baby is crying. / In the swaddling-pages / a baby," says Bill Knott. "'Don't cry. No Solomon's-sword can / divide you from the sky. / You are one. Fly.'" We move from baby to swaddling-pages to the threat of Solomon's sword dividing the baby not from itself but from the sky, then to the baby metamorphosed into the sky itself and told to fly. We remain in the present moment of the crying baby, but we are in touch with babies past; the baby Jesus in swaddling clothes, the baby who is being fought over by two women, each claiming to be its mother. And beyond this, we are given the possibility of flight, of a nature that is as indivisible as sky.

In poem-time, the present *accompanies* memory and eventuality; it is not left behind, since the very activity of the words generates the poem's own present no matter what tense the poet uses. The poem's activity in the consciousness of the reader is a present-time event which may, nevertheless, draw on his past, his expectations and hopes.

> All lives that has lived;
> So much is certain.

When Yeats says this in his "Quarrel in Old Age," it is more than salutary. It is an acknowledgment that the past is not a burial ground but a living fiber that informs and questions what is and will be.

I sit in a Montana café having a meal with my mother, who is visiting from Washington State. Suddenly she remembers a time when she was beautiful, when she had the power of beauty. I realize I never knew her in that time, though often she still acts from it, as from some secret legacy. I see that I have failed to make her know her present beauty, so she must return endlessly to that past—a reservoir. Even as I see her, I see myself, my own aging. I walk with her into "the one color / of the snow—before us, the close houses, / the brave and wondering lights of the houses." It has been snowing during our meal, and the houses have been transformed by a covering of snow, as though time in the form of snow has softened all contours, has fallen down about us deep enough, white enough, to put everything on the same plane spatially and temporally. The girlhood beauty of my mother accompanies us as we leave, gives the houses their brave and wondering lights, causes them to drift in a white sea under the covering of night.

Perhaps it is our very forgetting that allows these past images significance. If we remembered constantly, the time-fabric of our lives would remain whole and we would have no need of the poem to re-involve us in what was part of what is and may be.

"Forget! Forget it to know it," Robert Penn Warren says in his poem "Memory Forgotten."

> How long
> Has your mother been dead? Or did you, much older,
>
> Lie in the tall grass and, motionless, watch
> The single white fleck of cloud forever crossing the
> blue—. . . .
>
> How much do we forget that is ourselves—
>
> Nothing too small to make a difference,
> And in the forgetting to make it all more true?
>
> That liquid note from the thicket afar—oh, hear!
> What is it you cannot remember that is so true?

So Warren connects forgetting with what we feel to be true, the smell or the sound from afar that, if we knew its significance, would give us back some essential part of ourselves. He makes forgetting a positive accident, like the money found in a coat you hadn't worn for months, an accidental payload. The truth that we are is bound up with our partiality, our inability to hold everything of ourselves in memory as we go. Every time we remember some forgotten moment in a way that illuminates the present or causes the present to mediate some past, then the boundaries we thought were there between past, present, and future dissolve, if only for the time that is the poem.

It is believed that in the infant's first consciousness of the events and objects passing before him, he does not separate himself from them, but experiences his own identity simply as an endless stream of stimuli. His response to events is not so much toward as *in* them. The infant is immersed in objects, and their time in space continues with him, is infinite.

The Hindus have a name for this continuing or fourth dimension of "being across time." It is called the *Linga-Sharira,* that which remains the same in us though our cells change completely every seven years and we are not in fact the same in body that we were. Part of what the poem does is to restore us to consciousness of the *Linga-Sharira* which continues through change and which is immeasurable.

The poem, because it takes place at the point of all possibilities, in that it can intersect with all past, present, and future expectations, is able to accommodate this fourth dimension, the "something else" of the *Linga-Sharira,* which allows us to change yet to remain the same through time. "The same," in this instance, means as in an overview, so the total life is seen at the same instant as any one point of the life and we may say, This is she as she is, was, and will be.

Proust reminds us that "perhaps the immobility of things that surround us is forced upon them by our conviction that they are themselves, and not anything else, and by the immobility of our conception of them." The past and future are linked to our apartness, our identity as beings cut off from this original immersion in a time without succession. In that time, the time of the infant, there were no landmarks apart from us to signal our departure or arrival, our movement toward or away; no forgetting or remembering was then possible.

Even the stopped moment of a photograph paradoxically releases its figures by holding them because the actual change, the movement away from the stilled moment, has already taken place without us, outside the frame of the photograph, and the moment we see ourselves so stilled, we know we have also moved on. This is the sadness of the photograph: knowing, even as you look, it is not like this, though it was. You stand in the "was" of the present moment and you die a little with the photograph.

Octavio Paz speaks of the poetic experience as one which allows us to deny succession, the death factor. "Succession," he says, "becomes pure present. . . . The poem is mediation: thanks to it, original time, father of the times, becomes incarnate in an instant." The poem then represents an *overflowing* of time, the instant in which we see time stopped without its "ceasing to flow." It overflows itself, and we have the sensation of having gone beyond ourselves.

"Poetry," says Paz, "is nothing but time, rhythm perpetually creative." In the time of the poem we are held, not as the photograph holds, but as in a simultaneity of recognitions which wake us up in the middle of our lives. The poem causes an expansion of the "now." Archibald MacLeish's "Epistle to Be Left in the Earth" is a poem which expands the "now" by including the speaker's and the reader's deaths as encountered by those who live after.

> . . . It is colder now
>   there are many stars
>   we are drifting
> North by the Great Bear
>   the leaves are falling
> The water is stone in the scooped rocks
>   to southward
> Red sun grey air
>   the crows are
> Slow on their crooked wings
>   the jays have left us
> Long since we passed the flares of Orion
> Each man believes in his heart he will die
> Many have written last thoughts and last letters
> None know if our deaths are now or forever
> None know if this wandering earth will be found
>
> We lie down and the snow covers our garments
> I pray you
>   you (if any open this writing)
> Make in your mouths the words that were our names.

Part of the recent popularity of the writing of poems in prisons, grade schools, poetry workshops in universities, and the wards of mental clinics has developed from the sense that we are traveling too fast through a time which has fewer and fewer of the future-maintaining structures with which we grew up. I mean the structures of marriage, of the family, of the job as a fulfillment of one's selfhood. These allowed one to look ahead into the near and far future of one's life with some expectation of continuity, which is a part of one's future-sense. We now have serial marriages, separations between parent and child, as well as jobs that come and go as technology fluctuates even more crazily to accommodate a product-oriented society.

It may be that the poem is an anachronism of being-oriented impulses. It is an anachronism because it reminds us ironically that we stand at the point of all possibilities yet feel helpless before the collapse of the future-sustaining emblems of our lives. This has reduced us to life in an instantaneous "now." The time of the poem answers this more and more by allowing an expansion of the "now." It allows consequence to disparate and contradictory elements in a life. The "I," reduced to insignificance in most spheres of contemporary society, is again able to inhabit a small arena of its own making. It returns us, from the captivities of what we do and make, to who we *are*.

When the "now" expands, it includes before and after. The poem reminds us that the past is not only that which happened but also that which *could* have happened but did not. The future, says Ouspensky, in a similar way, holds not only that which will be, but everything that *may* be. He reminds us that if eternity exists at all, every moment is eternal. Eternal time is perpendicular at each instant to successionary time, which is time as we *misperceive* it. An example of an unrealized future enacted in a poem is Gene Derwood's "Elegy," where we read that the boy "lamentably drowned in his eighteenth year" will not fulfill the expectations of adulthood:

> Never will you take bride to happy bed,
> Who lay awash in water yet no laving
> Needed, so pure so young for sudden leaving.

All time is *during*. That is why it is so hard to exist in the present. Already we are speeding ahead so fast we can only look back to see where we have been. I once said to a group of students that the poet is like a tuba player in a house on fire. Crucial events surround him, threatening to devour, while he makes inappropriate music with an instrument that cannot help causing its serious manipulator to look ridiculous.

This speeding up of the time-sense in contemporary life, through the technology of mobility and through the disintegrative nature of human relationships, has affected the language of the poem as a time-enacting mechanism. The poem has begun to move in simple sentences, in actions and images more than in ideas, to speak intensely about the relationship of one person to another, to attempt to locate its subject matter or its speaker, if only during the time of the poem, very specifically at 142d Street on July 23, 1971. Many contemporary poems have opted for the present tense and a great suspicion has fallen over the past and future tenses. If they are used at all, they are converted into a present happening in order to insure immediacy. The sentences are simple perhaps because this slows the time-sense down and makes the language more manageable. Though some wonderful poems are being written with this pacing, I am often nostalgic for a more extended motion. It is no secret that the contemporary reader has begun to balk at the periodic sentence. The atrophy of even short-term recall in America has caused the mind to resist holding complex verbal structures. When my Irish musician friend tells me of singers who can sing hundreds of songs that have been passed on to them, I see how far we have come from this kind of memory.

The poem as time machine has inherited a heavy responsibility from these strains on the language and on the human figure's diminishing stature among its self-perpetuating creations. The poem is expected to tell us, not that we're immortal, but simply that we exist as anything at all except contingencies. It has the old obligations to carry experience memorably in the language, but with few of the formal structures to aid memory. Its voices have become a chorus of one, the personal "I" venturing as far as the patio or the boathouse. But as regards man's relation to time, the poem has shown itself valiant. I am no longer envious of Flash Gordon and his time machine. The poem is the place where the past and future can be seen at once without forsaking the present.

In a poem I consecrate all that forgotten life through memory, cast like a light on my life and the lives of others. The poet is the Lazarus of the poem, rising up with it. In the time of the poem it is still possible to find courage for the present moment. The life imagined in the poem has been known to affect the speaker, the reader, their sense of what can be salvaged or abandoned in a life. However, if we are like the blind man whose reality in the instant of "now" ends at the tip of his stick as he walks along the cliff, we must still believe in falling. The poem, for all its bounty, is a construct, and though the words in it may give the fiercest light, we cannot live there. Poems are excursions into belief and doubt, often simultaneously.

Mostly we are with the child peeling potatoes at the kitchen sink. We are too short for the view out the window except when we stand on the kitchen chair, which we are not supposed to do, but which we do. The time in the poem can be as useful as a kitchen chair, helping us to be the right size in a world that is always built for others. If I did not grow up to be a horse, I will not hold it against my life. I could not think fast enough to keep my two-leggedness from setting in. Still, I know there is a young girl in me who remembers the language of horses. She is with me in the time of the poem.

With all the modern time-savers, we have no better machine for the reinvention of time than the poem. I would not trade my least-loved poem for a Polaroid snapshot. The real time-savers are those that accommodate the mind, the heart, and the spirit at once.

The Poem as a Reservoir for Grief

As more and more of contemporary life is forced into the present moment, or NOW moment, there seem to be fewer mechanisms which allow the past to be fully absorbed and lived once it has "happened." It has become harder to experience grief since it is a retroactive emotion which requires subsequent returns to the loss over a period of time. For only through such returns may one hope for the very real gain of transforming losses of various kinds into meaningful contributions to our own becoming.

It is not simply release from sufferings we need, but understanding of loss and, beyond understanding, the need to feel, as in the word *mourning*, the ongoing accumulation of bodily and psychic communication which loss initiates in us. Here I am not only speaking of the loss one experiences in the death of a loved one, but of those diminishments of being which become known gradually too, as when child or parent or lover discovers piecemeal the signs of neglect and lost trust. Poems have long been a place where one could count on being allowed to feel in a bodily sense our connection to loss. I say *bodily* to emphasize the way poems act not only upon the mind and spirit, but upon the emotions which then release the bodily signs of feeling—so that we weep, laugh, are brought to anger, feel loneliness or the comfort of companionship.

What often happens early on with a death or other calculable loss, is that one has a feeling of shock which brings about an absence of feeling. We are cut off from our bodily entrance to the loss. We stand outside the loss and are pulled along into new experiences before we have had the chance to ask "what can this mean?" We may feel a kind of guilt because *we have not felt enough.* This can cause even more avoidance of the grieving process, so that the integrative steps that might be taken to bring the loss into some meaningful consequence in our lives are never attempted.

We have too, in this time of mass communication, the opposite cause of an inability to grieve—that one is asked to feel too much: we are asked to witness disasters claiming thousands of lives, numerous political atrocities, domestic brutalities, massacres in distant countries, and the rape around the corner. It is no wonder that a certain emotional unavailability has become a part of the modern temperament.

In such a world, poems allow a strictly private access to the grief-handling process, or, on another level, poems may bring one's loss into communion with other deaths and mythic elements which enlarge the view of the solitary death. It is as if the poem acted as a live-in church, and one might open the book of poems in order, through experiencing loss, to arrive at an approach to one's particular grief and thereby transform that grief.

The oftentimes failure of professional counseling, including psychiatry, to provide a lasting solace and a spiritual resource for those who need to grieve, is a failure of American societal attitudes in general. America is, perhaps, a country *almost* ready for grief, for the serious considerations and admissions, recognitions and healings of grief. I see the public and private reassessments of the Vietnam War as one of the recent signs of this new willingness and capacity. The building of the Vietnam War memorial restored, in a symbolic way, the memory of those Americans who died in that war. Currently there is a growing awareness of the possibility of nuclear holocaust, so that whole days are viciously intersected by fears of such proportion that we have few ways of addressing them. It is as if we have been propelled into a kind of before-the-fact mourning for the earth and life in general because our fears are so stupefying. It is a productive mourning, however, in that it has provided the energy to motivate many sectors of the country to take action against this threat.

In my own considerations of grieving I have begun to wonder if the ramifications of an entire society's inability to grieve might be more central to our problems than we have yet been able to recognize. For instance, one might consider the high divorce rate and its possible relationship to various kinds of unexpressed grief. Then too, the rise in other violences, especially those against women and children, should be mentioned.

The divorce rate relates perhaps more particularly to the grieving of an entire sex, the grieving of women, who have come to value themselves in new ways, and who, in many cases, must eschew entire lives lived in the dominions of choices made by others.

As a stop-gap measure for these ruptures in domestic matters, counseling and being counseled has become practically a national pastime, a place for assessment and change making. But it has not answered this deeper need of the individual to grieve because its motives are too future-oriented in the short-term sense.

I am reminded of my own disappointment with marriage counseling at the time when my second marriage was in a state of collapse. The counselor was sympathetic when I cried in the first session, but when I cried in the second and third sessions, she reverted to a very businesslike disapproval. I was not making "progress." I was not "forgetting" the attachments of the relationship quickly enough. I should have been able, within the space of three weeks, to leave grief behind and plunge ahead into My Own Life. But my life had been so intricately defined in terms of the "other" that the grieving could not be accelerated as she would have liked. Counseling may often be aimed at the practical—getting one to function *as though* the loss has been accommodated. And, of course, we do this . . . we act *as if we could* move on, and we do. But counseling or other "self-help" methods for grief handling often belong to what J. T. Fraser in *Of Passion, Time and Knowledge* has aptly named "the business present."

The business present, he says, "pays only lip service to past and future; its essence is the removal of tension associated with future and past, in sharp contrast to the tragic present with its wealth of temporal conflicts."[1] Fraser explains that the Tragic Present "involves continuities and hidden necessities," while "the business present is informed only of discontinuities, that is, of chance" (416). When things happen to us only by chance we are not encouraged to search for meaning. Chance is its own meaning.

Self-help books exist to help the seeker package the problem and thereby allow a quick solution. They are the hamburger stands of the soul. We are all familiar with the questions, warnings, and promises of their titles: "Who Do You Think You Are?," "The Hazards of Being Male," "How to Win Over Depression," and "How Not to Make Love"!

Mass communication, unlike poetry, is aimed at the shrinking attention span. Its messages, according to Fraser, are engineered "to make the material digestible with minimal effort and with no effect other, or deeper, than the one desired by the financial sponsor" (426). This describes how the business present wants to act upon language and consequently upon our lives. It wants to drive out the ambiguity of language which is the life blood of grief feeling and of poem making and reading.

> A green parrot is also a green salad *and* a green parrot. He who makes it only a parrot diminishes its reality.
>
> (Picasso)

So a diminishment of reality takes place when our experience is negotiated without ambiguity. What most often allows ambiguity to operate is an access to our past in a way that relives it in some fullness, so that it is not lost or left behind as dross, but is incorporated into the present.

What the business present encourages, as Fraser sees so acutely, is "the flight of the masses from the terror and *responsibility* of knowing time" (426, my italics). When we are told to settle a loss account quickly, efficiently, this often involves placing the experience in the old business file. We do this by relegating that experience to the past—the dead past. It was briefly relevant, but we must move on like good soldiers.

Poems, through ambiguity and the enrichments of images and metaphor, invite returns. Poems partake of the tragic and recreated present, while the business present continues to focus entirely on the NOW. But the time of the poem is multi-directional. It reaches richly into the past and forms linkages with the present and with other isolated pasts. The poem searches into the future. It reminds us of longings.

Poems restore our need to *become*, a capacity the modern self is in danger of losing. Fraser recognizes the tragic poet as "the free, time-roaming ambassador" (419) who assists in our becoming. The poem does not package or, like a trained seal, deliver the message. Its knowledge evolves. Its very ambiguities point to the individualistic character of artistic expression itself. This ambiguity permits the spectator to insert details of his/her own, niches of perception left undermined or open by the artist.

Poems often remake the grief-causing experience in terms of myth or analogy so that the unconscious and the conscious experiences of the speaker and the reader are enabled to meet. Myth mediates between the conscious and unconscious minds. It moves from ego release to psychic and spiritual embrace.

There are many poems one might turn to as examples of what I've been talking about—the elegies of Milton, Gray, Thomas, Yeats, Dickinson, Auden, the entire work of Rainer Maria Rilke, poems by Akhmatova and Tsvetayeva and countless contemporary American women—some whose voices are almost entirely elegiac in tone: Bogan, Plath, Glück, and Gregg. With so much to choose from, I don't introduce the poems I've selected with any sense of them as definitive except in their appeal to me at this writing for their particular ways of handling grief.

The first poem, by Galway Kinnell, typifies the power of many poets to move through the separations of grief into a state of embrace. "Goodbye" begins with the death of his mother. Kinnell told me a fact outside the knowledge the poem gives that might be useful. This was that he could not be at his mother's deathbed, much to his sorrow. The poem was written in order to absorb regret: "I swallow down the goodbyes I won't get to use. . . ." There is also the suggestion that there was unresolved anguish between mother and son in the line, "whatever we are, she and I,

we're nearly cured," as though the mother's death were
some closing of that case. The act of writing the goodbye
is perhaps what will afford the speaker the wholeness of
cure.

Goodbye

1

My mother, poor woman, lies tonight
in her last bed. It's snowing, for her, in her darkness.
I swallow down the goodbyes I won't get to use,
tasteless, with wretched mouth-water;
whatever we are, she and I, we're nearly cured.

The night years ago when I walked away
from that final class of junior high school students
in Pittsburgh, the youngest of them ran
after me down the dark street. "Goodbye!" she called,
snow swirling across her face, tears falling.

2

Tears have kept on falling. History
has taught them its slanted understanding
of the human face. At each last embrace the dying give,
the snow brings down its disintegrating curtain.
The mind shreds the present, once the past is over.

In the Derry graveyard where only her longings sleep
and armfuls of flowers go out in the drizzle
the bodies not yet risen must lie nearly forever . . .
"Sprouting good Irish grass," the graveskeeper blarneys,
he can't help it, "a sprig of shamrock, if they were young."

3

In Pittsburgh tonight, those who were young
will be less young, those who were old, more old, or more
   likely
no more; and the streets where Syllest,
fleetest of my darlings, caught up with me
and hugged me and said goodbye, will be empty. Well,

one day the streets all over the world will be empty—
already in heaven, listen, the golden cobblestones have fallen
   still—

everyone's arms will be empty, everyone's mouth, the Derry
   earth.
It is written in our hearts, the emptiness is all.
That is how we have learned, the embrace is all.

The time-sense of the poem is actively making an arena to
reexamine the speaker's loss of the mother. In the second
stanza the poem suddenly shifts to "years ago" and the im-
pulsive act of a student who runs after the poet to simply call
out a furtive "goodbye." Her weeping and her calling after
him enact the speaker's wish toward his dying mother—that
he could rush after, or to her, to say goodbye. The impas-
sioned necessity and simple beauty of that act are impressed
upon us through the superimposition of the past moment
onto the present.

Part 2 of the poem moves the voice out of the personal
realm into "history." The mother becomes "the dying." The
snow in the poem is a secret emblem of separation, of "disin-
tegrating" in the poem, of loss of connection. But paradox-
ically, goodbye in the poem is given *in order to restore* the
connection. The mind is seen to *need* the past, to wish to
continue and complete it until the present is no longer
needed. The present exists not for itself, as we often assume,
but as the place to resolve the past. This means that the cur-
rency of the present is not as powerful as we often assume. It
exists merely to facilitate the reliving of the past and, as Kin-
nell indicates, is "shredded" once the past is "over" or re-
solved. The present undergoes a reversal of importance here
according to contemporary life modes which recommend the
killing of the past in order to live in the NOW. But ironically,
once this killing happens, the NOW suffers a loss of conse-
quence and is not fulfilled.

As Kinnell approaches in imagination the Derry graveyard
where his mother is buried, it is her longings he addresses
first, linking her to a future embodied as "armfuls of flowers"
that "go out in the drizzle," as if they were candles whose light
had been extinguished by the gradual and natural element of
the weather—not downpour, but "drizzle" so we almost hear
the hiss as the flames go out, each with its little radius of

silence. The mother's body lies with "the bodies not yet risen," so the act of the poem is the raising of the mother (her death) into the human embrace. Her body is seen to return to the elements, in the graveskeeper's words—"sprouting good Irish grass." This physical actuality coexists with the "nearly forever" which brings together the temporal and atemporal at this point.

Then we return with the speaker to Pittsburgh, the scene of the young student's goodbye. But now the time span, the aging of the speaker and the student and those in the world at large are acknowledged: "those who were young / will be less young, those who were old, more old, or more likely / no more." The absence of that one caller who is now named tenderly "Syllest, fleetest of my darlings" is experienced as streets which "will be" empty. It's an imaginative living of those streets since the speaker is not there except as he recalls the moment of Syllest's catching up to him in streets where she no longer appears, as he also does not appear. Now the poet brings us physically closer to Syllest by allowing her to hug the speaker. We are moving closer to the longing for total embrace which impels the poem forward. Next, the speaker leaps from the emptying of particular and remembered streets to future streets: "one day the streets all over the world will be empty." The word "empty" moves us from the streets to the emptiness of arms, and now "everyone" begins to include a speaker who holds the past *and* the present. "Everyone's arms will be empty, everyone's mouth, the Derry earth." So at last, even the earth *will be* empty. The future exists as longing, but takes on a new palpability in the verbalization of it in the poem.

The end of the poem includes the reader, carries us into "our hearts," uniting the word *emptiness* with the word *all* so that the loss becomes enlarged. "All" has become the hinge which brings emptiness and embrace into conjunction. The last lines embrace but also release. Emptiness has somehow been carried into a fullness which *allows* release by virtue of an embrace.

It is written in our hearts, the emptiness is all.
That is how we have learned, the embrace is all.

This completion is the speaker's acknowledgment of the loss, having been able to bring together emptiness and embrace. Had Kinnell ended the poem on "the emptiness is all" we would have had an entirely different feeling at the end. But we are gathered back *into* the all, enclosed. The necessity of the embrace has been reinstated. This perhaps allows the speaker to return that embrace Syllest gives him in the past, and enables him to give the ungiven embrace to his dying mother, and finally to the "everyone" the poem admits at its close.

So it is the past which nourishes the present, allows the resolution, the grieving for the death the speaker could not attend. There is an undercurrent too in the poem of the speaker's own self-embrace. It's as though he also has had to say goodbye to that part of himself which died with his mother. He enters the "all" which is the union with others and with the earth and the spirit of the lost one the poem has been seeking. A symbolic accompanying of the mother's death does then finally occur.

William Heyen's poem, "The Berries," moves not toward embrace so much as toward loss experienced as a joy let go. Heyen brings grief to the point of joy through the sacramental acts of the speaker, who carries the gift of a jar of jam to a friend whose father has died of cancer.

The Berries

My wife already there to comfort,
I walked over icy roads
to our neighbor who had lost her father.
The hard winter starlight glittered, my breath
formed ascending souls that disappeared,
as he had, the eighty-year-old man
who died of cancer.

In my left coat pocket, a jar
of raspberry jam . . . I remembered
stepping into the drooping canes, the ripe
raspberry odor. I remembered bending over,
or kneeling, to get down under the leaves
to hidden clusters. . . .

Then, and on my walk, and now, the summer berries
made/make a redness in my mind. The jar
presses light against my hip, weight
to hand to the grieving woman. This gift
to her, to me—being able to bear
the summer's berry light like that, like this,
over the ice . . .

When I was a boy, the Lord I talked to
knew me. Where is He now? I seem to have
lost Him, except for something
in that winter air, something insisting on being
there, and here—that summer's berries, that mind's
light against my hip, myself kneeling again
under the raspberry canes.

By the fourth line of the poem we're made aware of the vast spatial dimensions of the universe: "The hard winter starlight glittered. . . ." Then the speaker's own breath becomes the breath of "ascending souls" as though breath made souls visible for that moment. This image is then connected with the particular death of the friend's father.

The picking of the raspberries, which the speaker is carrying as jam to comfort the surviving friend, comes back to the speaker in very rich, sensual terms. The berries "made/make a redness in my mind," and this enables them to continue as memory even as "the jar presses light against my hip." The gift giving becomes a gift to the self as well, in that the speaker is carrying, is the bearer of the summer's *light*, and so in this act unites summer and winter. Earlier in the poem, the act of kneeling and the secret, hidden nature of the harvesting (which refers also to the death of the eighty-year-old father) has connected the natural act of harvesting with the painful loss of the loved one. These coexist in a new proximity in the poem, thereby transferring to the death the idea of ripeness, of readiness for harvest.

The union of summer and winter has been moved, in the last stanza, toward the recognition of distance between a childhood closeness to "the Lord" and the adult loss of this spiritual closeness. So the loss of the friend has evolved into recognition of a loss of touch with God. But the winter air and

the memory of summer light in the berries restores an ambig-
uous closeness to the divine. The poem closes with the act of
kneeling, thereby suggesting a humbling of the speaker to the
gift of the berries—and the death. The death of the friend
has now been transformed, through an act of memory, into a
richness that includes gift and childhood and harvest, as well
as spiritual questioning. The emotional alchemy of this poem
is a restoration of order, the sense of naturalness and right-
ness, of childlike simplicity before those absent presences of
ripening berries, of one's God, and of a recently lost loved
one.

In a last example, Michael Burkard's much less linear
or narrative movement in the poem, "Islands of Feeling," en-
acts the disconnective effects of loss in its very method.
When, under the pressures of business-time we are seen to
endure rather than to *become,* time seems cut off from its tem-
porality, its ongoing arrival. "It no longer passes," Fraser has
observed. "It no longer completes anything" (419). As in Beck-
ett's *Waiting for Godot* we are marooned in a stagnant pres-
ent. Having come forward without memory, we are simply
prolonged. Similarly, in Burkard's poem, we experience
time cut off from its healing possibilities. The time unit
of the poem is "the moment" as in business-time. We are
made to feel the ways in which one moment is cut off irrev-
ocably from other moments until each becomes "an island of
feeling."

Islands of Feeling

Here are a few branches of
those condescensions you never wanted
me to speak of or mention,
a few examples
of how and when winter
spoke with such heart that I alone
fell. For a moment
no one else knew it. No one knew
this one example that keeps you

at a door in my mind, speaking
these feelings, these slight sharp blades

which accompany
speaking. O as you say:
I do not want to hear of that.

Even though as another, my friend
left me as he died and I walked
toward a winter door today, sharply,
then told myself to go back
and walk again. Any given call
that makes me walk has still
this lonely return to my friend.

I love you as no other, I would fall
asleep for you, as a few branches did,
as any act sharpens
a simple town,
a simple place lighted, left on for you.
Would I love as my friend
stepped through a few doors?
I would. These islands

condescend, come back to me—nothing
except their heart
and daily isolation
speaks for me. With your visitation
once I wanted
every answer, the kind an island
makes for me, a white reflection
of smoke off some ledge, some
view, which takes me by the hand,
walks down. Another moment

would sharpen, slapping at
such mind or deed. You bring to me
an island
of feeling. For that I cannot follow
I love.

In the third stanza the "you" avoids reception: "O as you
say / I do not want to hear of that." The death of the friend
(whether actual or emotional) is represented as "another." Is
this the death of yet another loved one? or does this mean
that the speaker himself has been changed by the death *into*
another? This is left ambiguous, but does not, I think, injure

our reception of the line intuitionally. We know there is a "dying" of some sort taking place, the dying of a friend, and that the speaker is developing an attitude toward that dying, that loss. The poem does not encourage the reader to "connect" images too surely and rather, rushes the syntax so as to dislocate our usual impulse to relieve tension through sequential assurances.

The poem begins to open up in the fourth stanza with an admission of love which is given *in spite of* "those condescensions you never wanted me to speak of or mention." The speaker seems to volunteer the self more fully here, and this becomes one of those "islands of feeling" the reader clings to because it allows emotional access to events not comprehended in a narrative and factual sense, events which the writer does not "condescend" to offer because to do so would invite an understanding more palpable than the true isolations of "feelings."

As the speaker concludes, he brings the reader to an island of feeling he calls love. The poem releases its grief into the word *love* only when it acknowledges that the speaker cannot *follow* the loved one, the friend, the you. Love then, seems to grow out of our *inability* to bridge one event, one feeling with another. So loving develops as a result of our island status, and not, as we normally assume, out of our coincidences with those we love or our accompaniments of them.

For Burkard, the moment keeps revising experience— "slapping at such mind or deed." This means that one may connect or follow only secretly, through acts of the heart, the mind: that which keeps the loss "at a door in my mind, speaking / these feelings, these sharp blades which accompany speaking." *Speaking* is what joins the words in time and space, words so sharp in their time-slicing power they are represented as blades.

The ending of the poem gives one a sense of the loneliness of the word *love,* its isolations, but also its generosity, as though love happens as a result of loss rather than in a reciprocation of feelings: i.e., I love *instead* of following because that is what is possible. Love becomes the only following the speaker can accomplish. Because of the completeness we associate with the word *love* it seems that love becomes almost *more* than following as the poem ends, so that the island affords a feeling which transcends the moment, the isolation of one person from another, or of the living from the dead, or of the speaker from the friend who makes a "visitation."

There is a mixture of regret and longing at the end of the poem, as if love takes on what cannot be lived in the impossibility of "following." Love paradoxically occurs in the absence of the loved one—"a lonely return."

I began this consideration of poems as aids to our grief handling by pointing out that poems allow imaginative returns to the causes, the emblems of loss—returns which do often involve regret and longing toward a hoped-for embrace. The poem may also transform grief by placing it in relation to rituals or natural cycles such as harvesting, or the return the poem makes may simply lead to a more complete experiencing of the disintegrating aspects of loss, its refusals.

By concluding with Burkard's view of our island status, I wish to return to the solitary and most often lonely act that the reading and writing of poems involves. It demands huge leaps of faith and audacity as a writer to ask that one be followed, be understood, felt—especially in the poetry of grief, because each loss is ultimately singular, an "only."

Poems engage our imaginations and emotions in a way that is particularly needed now, if we are, in our national and personal identities, to move from a state of being *almost* ready for the serious work of grieving to a true state of readiness. For it is the experiencing of grief which allows us to value fully those events, those people who are irreplaceable, so that, as Burkard says, we "love them as no other."

It is important that the inner nature of our beings be strengthened by the wisdom of our grieving. The scientists may tinker, the politicians may instruct us in the various ploys of moral unconsciousness, the physicians may delay death awhile with yet another treatment, but, until individuals maintain a responsible relationship to their own losses and changes, there will be no such thing as a hopeful future. For, like the Taoist description of the wheel in terms of the strong, empty spaces *between* the spokes, one's future depends not only on the visible spokes of the present, but also on those invisible elements from the past—those things we are missing, are grieving for and which we have forgotten and left behind in order to recover them again as new meaning, new feeling.

It seems important that grieving not be separated from other aspects of one's work toward a wholeness of being. It belongs there within the fabric of psychic, spiritual, intellectual, emotional, and intuitional perceptions through which we move. Because poems, as in no other function for which we use language, are able to carry the density of such a complex synthesis, they are the best and oldest forms we have for attending and absolving grief, for bringing it into a useful relationship to those things we are about to do toward a future.

NOTE

1. J. T. Fraser, *Of Time, Passion and Knowledge* (New York: George Braziller, 1975), 416. All further references appear in parentheses in the text.

Scarves! Echoes! Pavilions!

The Poetry of Laura Jensen

In a beautiful preface to his poems, the Irish poet Seán O
Ríordáin, who died in March of 1977, describes the child-
mind as it relates to poetry, perception, and being. It enlivens
an old idea: when we give ourselves over to the child-mind we
are most able to enter the appearances of the natural world.[1]
O'Ríordáin's preface presents without pedantry something of
the magic in Laura Jensen's poetry:

> What is poetry? The mind of a child? Imagine two people in a
> room, a child and its father, and a horse going past in the
> street outside. The father looks out and says: "There is Mary's
> horse going past." That is a telling. From all appearances the
> father has lost the horse because he remains outside it. Say a
> horse is a disease. The father does not catch the disease. The
> horse does not enrich the father's life. But as for the child—he
> apprehends the sound of the horse. He tastes the sound of the
> horse for the sake of the sound itself. And he listens to the
> sound getting weaker and weaker and falling back into silence.
> And he wonders at the sound and he wonders at the silence.
> And he apprehends the rear legs of the horse and wonders at
> their authority and antiquity. And the world is filled with hor-
> siness and the magic of reins. That is to be—to be under
> another appearance. And that, I think, is poetry.

Wonder, a key word, applies to Jensen's work both in the
sense of her ability to evoke amazement in the seemingly
ordinary and also as wonder*ing,* questioning of what others
take for granted. Jensen literally puts us under appearances
in "Cloud Parade," a poem which appears in both *Anxiety and*

Ashes (Iowa City: Penumbra Press, 1976) and *Bad Boats* (New York: Ecco Press, 1977). Its carnival atmosphere compels us to stand at attention, reseeing the earthly parades of our childhoods, those flat-on-the-back afternoons of fashioning animals and objects from the clouds, "attics and beds, men with moustaches / heels over heads." Then the magician's exclamatory "Scarves! Echoes! Pavilions!" and we are in a world in which even the smoke from the fireplace is "beautifully made, / in deference to the cloud parade." The world is infused with cloudness; our walking-around earthly pursuits are no longer the main event.[2]

Jensen's strong attachment to the work of various children's writers has perhaps helped sustain a simplicity of statement, a lightly moralistic tone, and a sense of being which repopulates the world by giving animals and objects back their power to act on us and to be dignified and humiliated by our actions.

Primary among these children's writers has been Laura Ingalls Wilder. Her books about pioneer life, moving by covered wagon from Wisconsin, where she was born in 1867, to Kansas, Minnesota, and the Dakota Territory, have been an inspiration to Jensen. Since these books were written for children, and since the child will continue to come up as we look at Jensen's poems, let me present the flavor of that world according to Wilder, this from the beginning of *The Long Winter:*

> Swarms of little white butterflies hovered over the path. A dragon-fly with gauzy wings swiftly chased a gnat. On the stubble of cut grass the striped gophers were scampering. All at once they ran for their lives and dived into their holes. Then Laura saw a swift shadow and looked up at the eyes and the claws of a hawk overhead. But all the little gophers were safe in their holes.

In this world, danger appears suddenly to the innocent who are yet able to dive safely into their holes, their places of comfort and safety. Wilder, as does Jensen, identifies acutely with animal and plant life to the extent that the protagonist takes on the consciousness of the gophers. Thinking of them underground, we enter the consciousness of sky and open ground with a sense of the intricate network of safeties these animals have prepared. Similarly, Jensen's poems are often involved in the building of comforts which accompany the anxieties that haunt her like the appearance of the hawk shadow on the open field.

Wilder's stories are full of real hardships on the way to rescues. There is the time, for instance, Laura and Carrie stumble through a blizzard to the warmth of their home:

> Laura sat stiffly down. She felt numb and stupid. She rubbed her eyes and saw a pink smear on her hand. Her eyelids were bleeding where the snow had scratched them. The sides of the coal heater glowed red-hot and she could feel the heat on her skin, but she was cold inside. The heat from the fire couldn't reach that cold.

This internal cold that cannot be reached by the heat of the fire gives some sense, I think, of the emotional center out of which many of the poems in *Anxiety and Ashes* were written. The activity of writing these poems might be compared to the way one must blow on one's hands in freezing weather while heading toward a hope of warmth. The revivals are momentary and need to be renewed since the cold is steady, the breath partial. Beside Wilder's bleeding eyelids, Jensen's motions are more subtle, as when she "forgets geriatrics" or notes in "In the Hospital" that the cups are "made in Occupied Japan."

It's hard for me to read this last phrase without irony since Jensen was herself at that time (Spring 1974) in the occupied Japan of the hospital in which that poem was written. She must have sensed during this time that the poems were a foil to that occupation, a way of preserving choice.

She brought out the first penciled version of "In the Hospital" on one of my visits to her there. As she read it aloud to me, other patients hovered in and out of the doorway, momentarily drawn in by the quiet of the voice carrying the words calmly the way a breeze ruffles again and again the sleeve of a curtain. I had the sense at that moment of something too humble and instinctive to call itself courage, though it had that affect. The poem seemed to me a very large and secret victory against the world of the adults, the doctors and prescribers, the occupiers.

The captive life of the patient resembles that of the child. There are the pill givings, the feedings, the blood takings, the various impersonal invasions of the body. "In the Hospital" keeps insisting on memory, that faculty so threatened and injured by a "treatment" known as "shock therapy" and still being administered in hospitals all over this country. Although not made specific in the poem, it is the memory of her grandmother's death which comes back to Jensen during her own hospitalization. Remembering that loss becomes a way of telling what endures, of accompanying the self with familiar presences:

> Breath was what you lost
> of her, that last moment.
>
> Her love returns to you,
> moment by moment, in the oval
> messages of snow, in the oval
> lips of cups. The curtains
> are a message of her veil,
> the glass the thin wall
> of her clothes, the drawers
> like the lives who used her cradle.

Forgetfulness is the pain, the fear through which Jensen discovers extremes of tenderness and performs unexpected transformations. The weather itself seems a message, the falling snow making visible the breaths of the absent grandmother. The snow, which reminds her of flowers, also reminds her that unseen beauties coexist with harshnesses *when we remember they do.* Memory then becomes a way of restoring, of returning the love of the grandmother to the self in an alien situation, the "answer to the answer to a prayer."

It *is* brutal that our lives come down to us "like a cord of firewood / burning," that is, already aflame with those inherited predispositions over which we fear limited control and the prospect of ashes. But phoenixlike in Jensen these ashes "sprout."

> Ash will sprout
> as the ash from the candle
> in the seed's heart.

The final vision of the title poem, "Anxiety and Ashes," is a mocking one in which "the match laughs / at the joke of the body, / nudges the wick, / and laughs." This laughter occurs also at the end of "In the Hospital" but with some resolution and less taunting:

> Didn't I always understand
> the snow and the laughter, the bay leaves
> of the cupboards resting in the snow.

The speaker up until now has been looking out a window toward a spectre, "the bent man and his / frosty plumes of breath." Then a potentially violent thing happens. The interior of the house, the cupboards with their store of bay leaves, are dumped into the snow, but in such a disarming way that it seems the cupboards are being received by the snow. The verb "resting" engineers a final vulnerability, the opening of the heart which the poem has been moving toward. Although the laughter here belongs to the speaker's helplessness during the occupation, it is also joyous and reflexive as the speaker's own triumph in delivering the contents of the cupboards into the snow. This is an act of truce:

> the truce between bones
> and the skin of your hands,
> the truce of these dark trees
> on the clean sheets of snow.

Breath is a hinge, spilling us beyond our wills, back into the larger air. Memory, closely allied to breath, returns us to that larger consciousness in which we are an extension of those who preceded us, making us "followers of air" and, by sound association, flowers of air.

Hearing this poem would put an end to this interpretive aboutness. Its pacing, the way it measures out the breath in the first stanzas, makes one aware of breath as a destructible containment. The two-word stanza "Night. Snow." inserts an un-avoidable calm. There is the mother-may-I progression of "a thought at a time, a world at a time," and the whispered diminuendo of "Mother I speak softly and father does not hear," which builds to the crescendo of the last two stanzas.

The interior sounds form a linkage, a hidden circuitry throughout the poem. The most insistent of these patterns is the long *o* sound which carries a moan inside the pulse of the poem, a pleading for the opening of the house and heart to the effortless snow, one's exposure before its overwhelming purity.

This is perhaps the most complex, successful, and auto-biographical of Jensen's poems in these books and allows us our closest view of the speaker. "In the Hospital" is an arrival poem because it confronts anxieties by transforming elements of fear, snow, loss of breath, loss of memory, loss of self into beauty. "Beauty is made by fear," Jensen says in a later poem, "Writing Your Love Down" in *Bad Boats*. As in this line, an aphoristic brand of wisdom begins to take charge in the more recent poems. Often the concrete partakes of the abstract and vice versa. That is, actual elements are carried into the unseen and conversely, the unseen moves into the elemental: breath into frosty plumes into snow, snow into flowers, snow into tears, into white cinders and in the reverse: lives into cord-wood, *forgetfulness* like a message on one of the *cups, love* in the oval *lips* of *cups,* the *glass* the thin walls of the missing grandmother's *clothes,* all manifestations of one another. Un-seen and seen, appearance and disappearance revive each other. So in "Baskets" we find the bird's color entering the basket woven near a river. The bird will fly away at the end of the poem in the speaker's own statement that she cannot fly.

Jensen often does various turns on the word "nothing" and the attempt, invariably, is to subdue the vacancy of that word. Just as often, she uses a negative to insert a positive. In "Animal," a poem which proceeds as a riddle, she reassures us that "nothing *is* too thin to endure the danger" . . . "even the snake / bakes on his own rock." The last verse of the poem identifies that keeper who is "cousin to the crow's collection" as comfort itself.

> I am that other animal,
> comfort. Everything,
> even the winds that threaten,
> come to me.

Comfort has become the controlling element by the end of the poem so it is a generosity when comfort receives the menacing winds, here become animal and needful.

Similarly, Jensen extends an animal personality to the ground in the opening lines of "Well Water," asserting again that these elements we take so for granted have wills and ambitions of their own. Even though personification and anthropomorphism have been poorly esteemed as poetic currency of late, Jensen manages to make it work most of the time.

> The ground has seemed to know more thirst
> than the short hair on its back called grass,
> ruffling to it more now, suspicious
> of drought and whispers through it, wind,
> closer to a pet of wet feathers,
> when the ground gets more than the grass.

The line "closer to a pet of wet feathers," is one of Jensen's more quirky constructions. The word "pet" here means that the grass is in a sour mood (a pet) because the ground, it suspects, will get most of the rain. We might also think of the ground as a pet, an animal to bestow one's affection upon.

Jensen's lyric jumps in the poems enlarge spatial and rhythmic possibilities although they also cause some confusion which unbalances the reader from time to time. Madeline DeFrees suggested that the mind in these poems is a solitary one, one used to allowing itself to range and therefore not always aware of its own jumps or, in company, when it has moved too quickly or forgotten to bridge a thought. Jensen accomplishes these leaps often with a statement such as "the swallow would like to help us all." Suddenly it seems as if the swallow *has* volunteered by the sheer impact of this saying. We even want to trust the swallow because, unlike us, he "has never mistaken a path for a river." The sheer excitement of the way a swallow moves might be an apt metaphor for the exuberance of Jensen's own jerks, sudden flights, and nervy flittering. We're taken inside the emotional world of the swallow when she tells us "excitement makes him sad," for it seems "that he has a troubled memory; / that he is too happy about flight." In these sudden shifts there is a constant "troubling" of the memory by the very structure of the poem. As with the swallow, if the memory is troubled, flight becomes disjunctive, too happy, that kind of glad-sadness akin to hysteria. This "too happy flight" carries an implicit criticism. Perhaps it's a part of the modern condition: the way we convince ourselves into false happiness in order to keep the motion up. Consequently we're thrown more and more outside memory and meaning. Jensen's efforts toward coherence in this "too happy flight" might be seen as a series of landings which release into the next consideration.

The use of the collective "we" serves as a gathering force in many of the poems and this gives a foothold where the movement is sudden. "We" remember "ghosting it / with headlights, water witching anywhere, / anywhere, and with a turkey wishbone." Here again this emblem of childhood becomes an implement of hope. In our desperation to find the wished for water we are handed a miniature witching stick in the turkey wishbone and made to see ourselves in that remembered state of faith when well water *could* be anywhere, when breaking the wishbone *could* affect one's future because it was believed. As readers we feel oversized and our childhood means of sustaining hopefulness becomes lilliputian. Some malicious joke has been played on us. One minute we are the gigantic Alice in a world of matchstick bridges; the next we are with those yellow weeds, lilliputian enough to be drowned by a puddle.

The apples of the last stanza involve a rather private reference to a poem of mine called "Apples From the Ground" in which I steal some apples from a landlady's backyard. The "you" then points to the dedication but also to the speaker who is in a self-accusatory mood.

> What you took in apples I took in handfuls
> from a watering can,
> the well water meant for the flowers.
> The smell of the gravel is as it should be.
> The rain is ahead of me already on the path.

That the water should be set aside, *meant* for the flowers, is a state of concern for other-than-self that I'm thankful to be returned to. We live in such a state of arrogance with the natural world that we tend to appropriate it; how right it is to remember that the water does not belong to us, that we are borrowers and takers. Luckily, the rain, like language, replenishes, is always ahead of us on the path, beyond our needs, our deservings and usuries. So the poem ends with nature balancing out the speaker's appropriation of the water. The well will fill again, which signals a restoration that the natural world takes upon itself.

The image of the well reappears in Jensen so often that it would seem to be a key to the emotional anxieties of the poems. Again, like Alice we might suddenly fall down one of these wells. As in the line from "Tantrum," "The body takes the throat / like an enemy tower," we are always on the verge of this takeover, this lapse in our own control in which we hear ourselves speaking from far off "as hail rattles on a board fence, / as the telephone wires / take the snow to be a mountain."

Hearing Jensen read in Chicago, I realized she sometimes leaves out entirely the event which occasioned the poem. "Hydrangia" is a poem, she said, about watching a fireworks show. The fireworks do not appear in the poem, except perhaps as the "harvest of flowers" in the poem's last line. In "Household," a farmer's wife sends a packet of needles with her daughter who is going to the city. It's possibly unclear that the speaker is the farmer's wife. Because the needles take on a personality and are "stubborn," the method is somewhat surreal: "a fingertip is sleeping in a thimble"; there is "a haystack of needles," "needles spending their lives now / forgotten from raincoats in a rush." This poem comments under its surface on the making of poems: "It is not easy to sew with an ignorant needle." Needle here could read "word." The poem proceeds to use words as if they don't know what they mean. It sews with an ignorant needle and the result is one of the most purely musical passages in the book, echoing children's riddles:

Once building a needle, once building a weed
was a young time, once, that leaves itself be
a wheedling eye, a thread of light
between ins and the reputable grasses,
their brass teasing eyes to believe.

If there were no trouble, borrowing,
the troubles would be in the rivers
and the rivers would be rivers
that the troubled find.

Here the language doubles back on itself, carrying us blindly
into the next stitch but arriving miraculously at a feeling of
wisdom beyond reason and sense, at a finding, but no ordi-
nary prosaic finding. The assonance and repetition are the
inner coherence that bind the seam.

Often in Jensen's poems the tone carries a naive spunk-
iness that reminds one of Dickinson and Marianne Moore, as
in "Two Poets at the Abandoned Farm":

The poets did not wait
for invitations. What could they have
said? See these vistas?
See how a house dies like a man,
with its boots beside the bed?

The house seems to have absorbed the absence of the farmer,
just as the cat absorbs the bird into its "well of feathers." Not
only do the poets not wait for invitations—they are, in fact,
trespassers—but they refuse to romanticize (with "see these
vistas") the loss apparent in the abandoned farm. The resto-
ration of such a place, they realize, is the hard work of patch-
ing a quilt; the work of the poet is no less matter of fact.

Bad Boats carries over many of the poems I've already spo-
ken of, but the new poems, as the title indicates, add a scold-
ing, ironically moralistic tone, as though a mother had ap-
peared on the scene. The loneliness of the poems is less self-
inflicted and seen to be the general condition, as in "Here in
the Night" where the speaker says:

> When I feel bad I wonder why they do not come
> to help me, why they let me go on this way,
> but who are they? And what are they, but alone?

A dog barking anonymously in the first line becomes personal in the last line, barking "as if it were caring for me." The speaker has the sense of other activities going on in adjacent apartments and this causes a dollhouse effect so that we view the aloneness and togetherness of the "they" at once, as though the front of the house were torn away.

I remember a conversation with an East Coast editor friend to whom I had shown this poem. He objected to "but who are they? And what are they, but alone" as sentimental. This word has come up again in relation to Jensen's reliance on repetition noted in a rather hastily taken view of the book in the *New York Times Book Review*. I want to suggest, perhaps dangerously, that this designation signals a very real difference in East and West Coast sensibilities as regards what is tolerable or "enough" in what a poem volunteers emotionally. My own return to the West after three years in New York State has underscored these differences. What in the East would be excess is in the West a sign of full-spiritedness, willingness. To admit the essential vulnerability of one's humanity is not an embarrassment or redundant, but rather the impulse to invite, to share, to feel.

I don't mean to insist on polarities which depend on such generalizations that the truth is blotted out by the exceptions one begins to advance. Nonetheless, I would protect the way Jensen's poems at such points speak directly out of the generosity in that sensibility one seems to find especially now in the West, one which still allows candor without cynicism. Perhaps this is a luxury and old-fashioned for readers in the East, especially in New York City where one walks about day after day embalmed in a great mass solitude. There one comes to appreciate terseness, economy of word and gesture, the look that scales a tower, the reluctance toward personal history, the regard for the complaint and for one's privacy.

If anything, I'd like to see the fullness in Jensen's poems enlarged upon. In the less successful poems one has the feeling of a scaffolding along which images collide and intersect precariously, and mystery sometimes withholds essential connections. Restraint is a large part of our excitement about what is given in the poems, but the nature of that restraint is still developing, and it appears to be getting more clearheaded in poems such as "Praise," "Patience Is a Leveling Thing," and "As the Window Darkens."

Jensen's poems continually invite the reader back. She manages a high degree of complexity and seems to break many of what have been thought to be the "rules." The passive verbs and simple syntax are deceptive. They cause an evasiveness ("Happiness is a thread to find" . . . "Happiness is one lucky clover") that eludes even as it defines. Jensen's use of repetition—"This is the time for it / this is the best time for it"—gives an eerie sense of the inevitable in such poems as "The Red Dog" and "House Is an Enigma." She is so animated by the presences in her poems that they seem almost to write themselves out of the surety of her consciousness. Their unpredictable movement is what delights. As in "Tapwater," the title poem of the Graywolf edition, most of Jensen's subjects are everyday, familiar happenings made consequential by a rare intimacy and mystery. They are full of riddles, music, childhood memories, and the ritual comforts that words can give:

> here from the garden of beliefs
> a garland of shells to circle ourselves.

NOTES

1. Since O Ríordáin wrote only in Irish, I have this translation thanks to Ciarán Carson, a young Belfast poet (*The New Estate*, Wake Forest Press).

2. For a while "Cloud Parade" was to be the title poem of the Penumbra book, but the shift to *Anxiety and Ashes* serves better since it reflects the need for the comforts many of the poems ultimately build.

Inside the Kaleidoscope
The Poetry of Michael Burkard

I find myself returning to the poems of Michael Burkard with persistent curiosity and durable pleasure. It is the pleasure of discovering a writer deeply engaged in the adventure of his selfhood in a way that is at once exclusive and inclusive (like any relationship between people). Access to Burkard's poetry depends to a high degree on the reader's ability to suspend the need for linear narrative, to go with the poem the way one might accompany a congenial kidnapper.

My involvement with his poems, I realize, borders on the obsessive. His *In a White Light* is a book I always carry with me on trips. I like reading the poems in public places as well as in the odd alone-times of journeys when there are strangers around me. A lack of interest from others is often good ballast. Improves the secret. Like my childhood fascination for kaleidoscopes, the poems seem to have shaken up during the time between my last reading of them and any new reading. New conformations leap to their surfaces. The colored bits refract in the mirror of my own interior. What I thought I was looking *at* looks *into* me. I dream into and away from the poems as I read. In this way the text becomes a kind of pre-text for self-journeys.

The poems in Burkard's new book, *Ruby for Grief,* will succeed or fail for the reader on the basis of whether or not the voice and patterning of image-montages in the poems engender sufficient trust for the reader to continue without "a feeding" ("Everyone wants a feeding"—"Gaslight"). Readers who are new to Burkard's work will, I suspect, feel somewhat like Hansel and Gretel, who witness with anxiety birds eating the crumbs of bread that were to lead them home. Home is a safe return they might have to delay indefinitely. In fact, this delay is an integral part of the strategy to lead the reader somewhere unexpected.

> This is the law of enjoyment, that pleasure does not have an even tenor, for this begets loathing, and makes us dull, not happy.[1]

> The poetic text of the lyric emerges from a crisis that it somehow both prolongs and attempts to resolve.[2]

Burkard's poems are "attempts" in the courageous sense of that word. Resolution is sometimes aborted in favor of satisfying a pattern, and meaning derives from this satisfaction of returns and from a strong musical impulse. The poems are "approaches" that invent their own configurations toward, into, around, and away from the very passages they make. As Jackson Pollock describes his more radical process of obliterating entire paintings, we glimpse a kind of extravagant freedom which involves un-creating as much as it does creating:

> Sometimes I paint a picture, then I paint it all out. I do that because I want to . . . because I like to change my mind so often.[3]

Over the past eleven years of reading Burkard's poems I've kept up a dialogue with myself on the nature of his work by making notations in the margins as I've read other diverse and often nonliterary sources. These have served as personal clues to his method or attitude. The notes read: "Michael's work?" or "M." or "Burkard!" or "What Burkard's doing?" The question mark is important to my offering of these passages. To apply them narrowly would be a mistake. Only a few notations point to individual poems. I see these "found passages" working more like propositions that might daydream their way through one's reading of Burkard's poems, attaching where they will, leading the way fire leads when you stare into it until the mind reaches out.

In an essay entitled "Feeling into Words" in his *Preoccupations,* Seamus Heaney tells the story of having witnessed a "diviner" who used a forked stick to discover well water. My own father was such a "diviner" in Oklahoma. When he came to the Pacific Northwest he had occasion to offer his neighbors the use of this peculiar receptivity to the natural elements. On one occasion when I was with him walking through a man's field, I saw the rod dip sharply in his hands as he came to the place where the water was later located, deep under the ground. "The diviner," says Heaney, "resembles the poet in his function of making contact with what lies hidden, and in his ability to make palpable what was sensed or raised." The curious thing about Burkard's work for me is that not only does he rely consistently on his powers as a diviner, he also asks that the reader become a diviner, so that much of the "making palpable" also rests with the reader. In Heaney's essay the water diviner or "dowser" is an example of someone who uses pure "technique."

> Technique, as I would define it, involves not only a poet's way with words, his management of metre, rhythm and verbal texture; it involves also a definition of his own reality.[4]

The difficulty readers have with writing that relies on divining techniques comes perhaps from the assumptions made about this act as "gift" and therefore not *given* or possible for all. Thus, the reader of such poetry may feel disqualified.

> You can't learn the craft of dowsing or divining—it is a gift for being in touch with what is there, hidden and real, a gift for mediating between latent resource and the community that wants it current and released. (Heaney)

I misread this final phrase as "the community that wants *its* current released," which is one of the functions a diviner of words does perform, the release of the hidden energies of the community—its "current." I might say here that I always try to use my misreadings of texts as well as my readings, and this is a valuable skill to have in reading Burkard, even though one is often unsure as one proceeds as to what constitutes a misreading. One may read far into a poem with the gnawing sensation that the poem's intent has escaped. "Intent" undergoes such fluctuation in a Burkard poem that finally it ceases to be the reader's energizing concern. What then replaces intent?

> If a man is incapable of getting for himself the intuition of the constitutive duration of his own being, nothing will ever give it to him, concepts no more than images. Here the single aim of the philosopher should be *to promote a certain effort,* which in most men is usually *fettered by habits of mind* more useful to life.[5]

Perhaps the method of these poems then acts similarly, to "promote a certain effort," and the extremities of that effort actually serve to unlock the strictures of our habit-mind.

> The seminal excitement (in the making of a poem) has to be granted conditions in which, in Hopkin's words, "it'selves, goes itself crying / What I do is me, for that I came." (Heaney)

For me, this insistence on the mission of art as inextricable from the search for being, as a giving of the writer's one and onlyness in that search, informs Burkard's stance in the poems. In his work, the assumption is that each person's peculiarly individual approach toward language enforces the need among us to become more intuitive readers, reaching new heights of sympathetic attentiveness with each other and with language.

In recent years one of my ways of teaching the reading of contemporary poetry has been to offer at the start of the class what I consider to be the poles of accessibility: poems by William Stafford and poems by Michael Burkard, in that order. Stafford poems encourage the reader to feel that he/she can expect to succeed without too much effort in following the speaker in the poem, both on a literal and on a metaphorical level. Burkard's poems perform more as riddles on what might be called "the oracular level."

> Traditionally an oracle speaks in riddles, yielding its truths in disguise, offering its insights cunningly. (Heaney)

These are both "ways," and pleasure will come to the readers of Burkard's poems once they have accustomed themselves to the effortless-effort the poems require, a suspension of the need to be located solely in terms of conceptual intent or "usable" meaning in the sense that one could address the poem's "aboutness" and assume clarity of intent.

Recently in an old notebook I came across a couple of paragraphs I wrote back in 1975 in order to introduce Burkard at a reading in upstate New York:

> In Burkard's poems the words are used as gestures—as the mime uses his arms, hands, and total body to simulate action and contact with objects. That is, the words don't act as separate units, but as phrases of motion which approach an invisible articulation of human events and emotions. It is the *sequence* of motions which arrive and not the individual motions. That is, if you turn away your head during a mime show, you interrupt the *path* of the images, and it is difficult to reenter on the strength of a single gesture. This points up the necessity for an intense focusing of the attention in one sense—but at the same time, a willingness to suspend the need for conclusiveness in the overall experience. If the viewer (reader) fails on either account, the encounter will fail him or perhaps it would not be ingracious to say *he* will fail the encounter.
>
> There are those who will be quick to say that an art which requires so much from its audience is an incomplete and lesser art than that which is immediately accessible or accessible in ways which require less tolerance or persuasion. But this is like indicting the moon as a lesser phenomenon than the sun because it does not warm the chair where you sit on your porch. I have sat all day and all night at a window and both the sun and the moon came there. There was no sound, but I have known them both, not because they were there, but *I* was—not because they spoke to me, but that I was *with them as they were.*

Rereading these notes I felt Burkard's poems had come a long way from needing the elaborate rationale I was offering the audience at that time. The poems have become more accessible. It seems now that my students don't have as much difficulty entering his poems as my colleagues do. This makes me wonder if this gain in accessibility has as much to do with a new permissiveness (laxity some would say) in language use, as it does with Burkard's own movement toward a more lyrical mode and away from his earlier long meditations such as "Sometime in the Winter" and "The Rafts." There were lyrical passages in those poems too, but the reader perhaps had more difficulty orienting and redirecting attention in those more sustained efforts. It could be that, as with Ashbery, the chance methods used to generate verbal movement have been given new assurance by tonal, syntactical, and voice elements, so that the poems no longer erode the reader's trust so easily. Perhaps the poetry audience in America is also developing more tolerance of the difficult. After forty years of what Josephine Miles has called "the poetry of clean edges, Wallace Stevens' dish of pears, William Carlos Williams' red wheel barrow," maybe readers are ready for poetry that is more strenuous of access, such as Jorie Graham's work—work which uses a high degree of abstraction; there is also a resurgence in the study of Pound in universities and a return to an interest in prosody. Geoffrey Hill, a difficult English poet, is also finding readers in America.

Contemporary poetry readers have been somewhat prepared for the difficulties of Burkard's method by poetic devices they've become familiar with, such as "leaping," the gift of volition to objects and their displacement in the environment by the Surrealists, the forcing of syntax in the work of Ashbery, and collage techniques in Duncan and Moore. I believe enough has already been said in connection with Ashbery's work about the influence of the Abstract Expressionists, so I would rather point out some related developments in film.

Eisenstein's *Potemkin* and Robbe-Grillet's *Last Year at Marienbad* have become landmark experiences as far as informing the viewer's intuitive willingness to approach narrative and image reading in a less linear way, using instead the disjunctive techniques of montage and plot elision to build emotion and meaning.

In my own involvement with experimental filmmaking I have come across commentary on the film work of Joseph

Cornell which informed my thinking about Burkard's writing. Cornell, an artist known primarily for his elaborate box constructions, also reedited old films, adding scenes from other films and revising the original content, tone, and rhythm in his new version. The results were what often happens naturally in the continued showings of a film print:

> . . . accidents of deterioration in which passages are damaged in rewinding, strange ellipses which occur in their repair. (Sitney)

What Cornell performed was a "deliberate mismatching of shots." As in film montage, the power of Burkard's poems is generated by the same mismatching of images or phrasings so that meaning often derives from what is left to our imagination, or from what feels even somewhat wrong.

> The "invisible" event gives meaning to the otherwise unfocused fears, anxieties, and intimations silently mimed by the heroine throughout the film. (Sitney)

The sort of questions that might be asked about such an experiment are: Is this portent without content? Or content which is reduced to portent? Perhaps when portent overshadows observable content, the portent itself *becomes* content. The usual roles are reversed and content becomes amorphous; portent—a prolonged foreshadowing or forward leaning into expectation and omen—becomes the compelling agent. One reason that portent has overwhelmed content may have to do with a change in our time perceptions. The present moment has come to seem both overloaded and empty at the same time. Cornell's theory of the imagination describes "a collapse and failure of the present, which brings with it a poignant and powerful compensation" (Sitney). For Cornell, this compensation results in a nostalgic prolongation of the past. It is given more portent, as though it continued to have a present happening even as a past moment.

In Burkard's poem "A Conversation About Memory,"[6] the act of memory fails both to inform the present fully and to maintain the entire fabric of the past. "All that past is now conclusive," the speaker says. It is conclusive because the present can't change it and it has become too cumbersome and partial (because of forgetting) to move into a present significance. Portent, in this instance, is the tattered remains of memory which intersect unpredictably with present moments.

Ashbery and Burkard have a similar investment in the moment as the time unit in which we are compelled to live, but their ways of making us feel its precariousness are quite different. Ashbery makes us swim for it, building up constructs that detour into tributary movements of thought and mental sensations of the lost and overfull present moment which has just streamed into the next moment. Burkard uses this method in "A Conversation about Memory," duplicating the inability of the linear verbal account to keep up with movement in time and memory. But Burkard isolates both past and present moments more—"keeping parts of the road lit, interminable 'parts' because there is no returning to their location"—alluding to the fact that once the present falls into the past it becomes mobile in relation to other past elements. In order to remain significant enough to be remembered, a new memory may attach itself to events which happened much earlier in linear time, thereby compounding earlier happenings with new ramifications. Memory-time then carries an agonizing multidimensional aspect; in its fragmented urgency—"a strange kind of wreckage"—it is fraught with attempts to unify and to articulate: "This is the third time you have tried to speak to you."

> Inner duration is the continuous life of a memory which prolongs the past into the present, the present either containing within it in a distinct form the ceaselessly growing image of the past, or, more probably, showing by its continual change of quality the heavier and still heavier load we drag behind us as we grow older. Without this survival of the past into the present there would be no duration, but only instantaneity. (Bergson)

Burkard seems to resent the responsibility placed upon memory to give continuity and dimension to the "now" moment, even though he realizes at the same time that it's all we have.

The telephone which is disconnected, torn from the wall, in "A Sideways Suicide" represents an act of anger directed at the telephone voice of memory which can ring the speaker up at any moment with new-old data (a grief-causing mechanism). Nevertheless, the speaker continues to talk into the dead telephone as if he were on record, denouncing "authors," those writers who would falsify loss with words like "departure": "authors are assholes, the rain that is lost is / memory that is lost, like you are. . . ." He wants the loss to bear its finality. The solution to this irrevocable loss is to "walk in a very local direction"—which could mean that he intends to stay close to the present. But perhaps he also means to stay close to the self and through both these acts thereby "revenge the change / that memory brings, as it must bring change, as it changes." So in the end, the "revenge" is a hopeless act, since memory will continue to revise itself and to inflict itself on the present. But the speaker's verbalization of revenge gives the impulse against memory's implicit violence a doomed yet courageous aspect.

Ruby for Grief, with its preoccupations about the action of memory on selfhood, reveals Burkard's metaphysical and intuitive orientation toward the kind of discourse Bergson was proposing in *An Introduction to Metaphysics.* Bergson described metaphysics as "the science which claims to dispense with symbols." This is accomplished through "seizing without any expression, translation, or symbolic representation," that is, not through conceptualizing, but through intuitional acts:

> By intuition is meant the kind of intellectual sympathy by which one places oneself *within* an object in order to *coincide* with what is *unique* in it and consequently inexpressible. (Bergson)

> . . . intuition is an *irrational* (i.e., perceiving) function. In so far as intuition is "hunch," it is not the product of a voluntary act; it is rather an involuntary event, which depends upon different external or internal circumstances instead of an act of judgment. Intuition is more like a sense-perception, which is also an irrational event in so far as it depends essentially upon

objective stimuli, which owe their existence to physical and not to mental causes.[7]

Again and again we see instinctual coincidence at work in the use Burkard makes of his materials. Signification is no longer the main purpose of words; instead they indicate, they haunt, they reflect.

Burkard's poems have always displayed a reliance on the intuitional workings of the mind, those mechanisms of understanding available to us at the unconscious level in dreams or at times when we are inexplicably in touch with an inner voice in such a way that we act out of it without consciously reasoning, yet with a surety that carries its own knowledge. At these times we are meeting experience on a level where thought and instinct are indistinguishable. Movement occurs through a synthesis of unconscious or partly conscious data which informs action before reasons become available.

As in our dreams, the images of Burkard's poems are such that we can't be sure of their interpretation. As Jung states, "In such a situation all one can do is accept the discomfort of ethical doubt—making no final decisions or commitments and continuing to watch the dreams" (Jung). The story of Cinderella that Jung goes on to tell is a fable in which agents of intuition make a physical appearance:

> . . . when her stepmother threw a heap of good and bad peas in front of her and asked her to sort them out—she began patiently to sort the peas, and suddenly doves (or ants in some versions) came to help her. (Jung)

These "helpers" are emissaries of the unconscious, and they represent "impulses that can only be felt in one's body . . . and that point to a way out."

In "Ledger," Burkard sets up his attitude toward memory—"There is no record of us, my darling"—which suggests a rationale for his intuitional method when he speaks of "a name with a scrawl for its final half." That is, since the record keeping of the memory is fallible, our past and therefore our present is always only partly legible. Just as we proceed with partial evidence of our past (what we haven't forgotten) we proceed with the articulation of that past as though the language is, to some extent, forgetting its own referential base in the past, its link with the very objects and events it has been charged with recording. The naming function of words is seen to fail in the poem: "Heartbeat, there is no record of, mention of us, notation for us. / No white name for stone, / no name written within the stone. / No white name, no white stone." Since names are all given to the unnameable, they are *in process* like everything else, changing. The name with a scrawl for its final half is a more honest representation of what each word is doing, its refusal to close, to designate. Because the word's concluding half is obscured, we are invited to guess in context; so any word's relation to the context is the only way it can be interpreted and then, not with surety, but as it will *change* each time you look at it and try to make it out.

> . . . a word resting on nothing, which must end and begin again of its own accord at each instant. (Bergson)

In some of my classroom attempts to bring new readers to Burkard's poems, this guesswork is what has most often been resisted, resented. And indeed, the argument goes, "How are we to know that this writer is not simply throwing feathers in the air? After all, anyone can make us guess." The fact is that *not* everyone can make us guess and *continue to guess* with a feeling of treasure just out of reach, but with enough clues to make the continued attention worthwhile. This is where the artistry of Burkard's work comes in. How does he engender the trust and willingness to guess even though there is no "payoff" in the sense of statement or conclusiveness? It is as if the words were blind and had to substitute an almost tactile awareness. The effect is sensually provocative, dangerous, and therefore fascinating. The intimate tone of the voice in the poems also establishes trust. This voice is like a psyche which is being bared to us. It is invitational and secretive at the same time—"then I make some private / and selfish demand for secrecy"—"Is generosity / so / privately handled a good thing?" ("Ruby for Grief"). The reader is baited and not made privy to the secret nature of the investigation except in coded form.

Attempts to decode are frustrating even for the speakers in the poems because "intentionality" is oracular, given to riddles: "Are omens / which take the form of memories immersed in water a good thing?" ("Ruby for Grief"). This unknowing involves the reader in a "lapping," wavelike motion toward and away from the text. Approach, touch, withdraw, build, approach. Memory itself is identified as "an omen" because of the way it causes past events to ignite in present moments so that, "if I got up and / went walking I would find imaginary omens everywhere" ("Ruby for Grief"). The reader may or may not decipher the message, but since the clues are without "result" or preferred arrivals, "getting it" is a mistaken direction. *Going with* is more important than "getting it," and the "with" implies that the reader must exert more intuitive concentration than rationality or analytic sleuthing. Our need to "get it" has to do with the way the rational mind works: "Our mind has an irresistible tendency to consider that idea clearest which is most often useful to it" (Bergson).

This impulse toward "usefulness" has begun to be frustrated, not only in our experience of nonrepresentational art, but in some areas of human relationships as well. A description of the refusals of the "new woman in recent fiction" in the *New York Times Book Review* spoke in a humorous vein for me in ways I associate with Burkard's aesthetic:

> In the manner of certain recent composers, she denies any "implicative harmonic relationship" with men . . . prefers instead the *phenomenological investigation of her own processes*. To appreciate this new woman, men must learn to forge an *esthetic of frustration*, make do with a provocative discomfort, substitute conceptual speculation for romantic or erotic daydreaming . . . the new woman's suitors must cultivate a taste for *the tensions of blocked inference*. . . .[8]

It is an unlikely set of instructions for appealing to a readership, and although I offer it in a spirit of play, I do think the idea that these poems of Burkard's need suitors hits close to the fact. *Webster's Dictionary* defines a suitor as "one who petitions," "one who seeks to marry." To give suit is "to meet the needs or desires of." So in the case of the reader and the writer, the roles have been reversed, with the writer asking the reader to court the text, to discover what the text desires. The reader is asked not to employ the services of the text for a set of already designated needs imposed upon it by the reader.

In *The Pleasure of the Text,* Roland Barthes takes rather the opposite approach, speaking for the reader's rights: "The text you write must *prove to me that it desires me.* This proof exists: it is writing. Writing is: the science of the various blisses of language." But then Barthes goes on to define bliss in such a way that one realizes that his idea of being "desired" or of "desiring" is as seemingly perverse to the mythical "intelligent reader" as are the needs of the "new woman in fiction." "Pleasure/Bliss: the meaning will be precarious, revocable, the discourse incomplete."[9] Barthes sees neurosis as instrumental in the formation of reader-writer desire—neurosis not in the sense of "mental health," but in the existential sense of one's "fearful apprehension of an ultimate impossible." He makes further distinctions as far as the difference between pleasure and bliss:

> Pleasure can be expressed in words, bliss cannot. Bliss is unspeakable, inter-dicted. I refer to Lacan ("What one must bear in mind is that *bliss is forbidden to the speaker,* as such, or else that *it cannot be spoken except between* the lines.") With the writer of bliss (and his reader) begins the untenable text, the impossible text. (Barthes; my italics)

An aesthetic which works on the faith that what has been forbidden to the speaker will be apprehended between the lines must expect at the start its Tallulah Bankheads: "There's less in this than meets the eye" (her comment on Abstract Expressionism, in Lucie-Smith). Because the text of a Burkard poem is "incomplete" in the ways I've been suggesting (which is its own completeness), the reader-suitor will have to play his hunches, some of which will be fruitful in terms that were not anticipated even by the text, although the text has provoked them (text as pretext). The object of these poetic texts is not containment then, but *release of potential.* It is perhaps the difference between dressage and riding bareback. Burkard is not an "author" because he refuses to take possession of his creation in the sense of becoming a "producer," one who "yields up," who "performs."

Signs of the intentional incompleteness of the reader-writer transaction are visible in most of the poems in *Ruby for Grief.* Burkard's view of selfhood is tenuously vested in memories which he strives to reencounter through the poems. To kill memory would be to kill self, yet as the memories enter words they defy "meeting," become elusive and incomplete. The advantage of this incompleteness is that it allows an extension of the sensual possibilities of language constructs, a widening of the view in which one may "change from an initial level of random mixed-upness to a patterned mixed-upness."[10] The job of the artist in such a work is the patterning of these possibilities. This patterning will have inflections without advocacy in some instances. At other times a preferred direction will evolve. In some of Burkard's early writing he seemed to be equalizing his efforts in a way which did not allow emotion to act very visibly. In recent work, however, we are often directed by the emotionality of the speaker, his outbursts—"I'd rather be stored / in the bow anyway (all the better / to see the fuckers removing their golden shoes)" ("From the Heavy Sunlight")— and candid admissions—"I don't ever want to love you . . ." ("The Parallel"). There is a self-assertiveness that causes the reader to feel that the speaker is invested in an urgency at least tonally available, *volunteered.* This emotional inflection is flirtatious, an incentive to proceed at an intuitive level, as the writer himself has proceeded.

"The Boat" illustrates the intricate patterning of sound structures which promotes a feeling of harmony in the midst of chaos. Rather than entering the tedious "aboutness" and referential hedge hopping it would take to convey my involvement with the interiors of the poem, I would like to offer the graphic representation of marks I made on the poem as I read it:

using prismatic action of words moving through context

Self alone can supply its worth

Transference of identities

Key to his patterning method

points to money?

rhymed words refracting off each other

Since it didn't matter that I had gone home I didn't
think to ask after myself -- for no one could bring
more money to me than I had for myself -- and here
in this ink I could safely say the ink and the few
wooded stars matter most, they mix without any
seeming intention and shift a few wooded feet
above the water, so their prisms are variously red,
and some green, and white and refracted in regular
intervals. The money made a different sense of the
refractory, and offered this as much "I am starving,
I am blue." Well, I had wanted to haunt various different
corners also, but couldn't see so much taking even time
for food, let alone eating alone The boat had contracted
nothing much I had a feeling for: the streets were
water, for sure, and the kaleidoscope had indeed taken
a false matter into another corner: it kept muttering
a more different and difficult sense for itself than
any I had remembered. Otherwise I would not have brought
mother along, I would not have had her And as for her
parrot, well, the parrot could stay topside the whole
voyage, as far as I cared. The boat reddened with nothing
so much as memory, and turned toward me. But it kept
itself from speaking, said nothing. And so ensured me
of the guarantee that I myself am not ready for such
memory, I can't say what it is, and so ensures me
of false hopes, far stars, a cold voice wise from sleep
which utters something like "I refuse" -- utters just
about any kind refusal. Drifts home, endlessly home,
hated and endlessly home.

not ready to know where it's going? what it has passed through keep refuses to record

The "I had" repetitions in the poem insist on the loss the
speaker is suffering, a loss that is not defined, except as
nuance, its "hadness"—"I can't say what it is." The loss re-
volves around the "refusals" of the speaker and also possibly
the way in which remembered experience comes to us "vari-
ously," mixing "without any / seeming intention." Neither the
mission nor the progress reports are clearly available. Bur-
kard's narrative style applies itself to this retroactive phe-
nomenon of memory. This mixing of before and after, of
prisms of attitude and feeling, revises the event and us with it.

The recurrence of the *u* sound, which is picked up in
"mother" and in "refusal," is a steady undertone in the poem.
It alternates with a full *o* which is anchored in the title word
"boat." The *u* sounds have the effect of an inaudible cry

which perplexes the conversational tone of the history being given—the history of what turns out to be a "hated" boat that is drifting "endlessly home." The boat is hated because it refuses—refuses control or to be told what it is and where it is to go, hated also because of its drifting. These are descriptions of Burkard's narrative method, his "drifting" from one event to another.

> It is certain that there has been this thing prose and poetry and narrative which is roughly a telling of anything where anything happens after any other thing.[11]

Anything may follow any other thing in the telling, regardless of how it occurred in linear time. As with painters like Magritte, *thought* is what animates and orders the world. Words, in this way, both contradict and coincide with the realities they designate, as in Magritte's famous assertion, "This is not a pipe," across a painting of a pipe. In his painting, "The Use of Words," two "virtually identical and amorphous blobs of paint are labeled "Mirror" and "Woman's Body" (Lucie-Smith). It is verbal gesture which overshadows "fact" or the "it" of Burkard's poems.

The parrot in "The Boat" reminds one of language which keeps insisting that it is relevant in all circumstances. An inappropriateness is implicit in the language fragments (like memory bits) which a parrot might volunteer whenever it receives a stimulus or acts on its own urge. Parrot language is frozen language, frozen memory—language which does not "live" in context except through its inappropriateness. This language belongs "topside" because it is antithetical to the true language, which is the interior language. It is significant that the parrot belongs to the mother, since this would indicate that the parrot and mother share the unyielding aspects of language which do the record keeping, the score keeping of one's life—the judgmental, law-giving aspects of memory. Memory has everything and nothing to do with what the parrot says, is *taught* to say. Parrot language represents the language one is given to apply to one's experience, while boat language, which "kept itself from speaking, said nothing" and which speaks *by* drifting, is the unspoken language the self alone can invent. These interior language structures may be false in terms of record-keeping language—"false hopes, far stars and a cold voice"—but they are "wise from sleep," wise perhaps because sleep is associated with a voice which refuses to conduct interior understanding with an exterior language, wise also because it has forgotten enough to be able to initiate change. One of the prime efforts then of Burkard's poems is to invent a way to force the parrot language he has been given to respond in a more vital way to his interior experience and the past. The manner in which the word *home* is emptied of its usual symbolic content (comfort and reception) by the end of the poem is a good example of the sorts of necessary divestments language often undergoes in Burkard's poems.

In some poems, words take over functions from other words. In "Study for Orange and Black," a "self-query" becomes "a stag" and "the stag" then becomes "the loan." Throughout this transaction the associations of each word are "loaned" in the developing context to others. The effect is a blurring of borders between words. They are not allowed to contain. They ride piggyback and travel on each other's initiatives. Even as nouns they may become "gradually abstract." Neither loans nor stags nor donkeys will read at a purely symbolic level because of this shifting of identities *within* the naming word. The stag is the image which clings most steadily to its association with the wild, the exotic, the miraculous event which the speaker was supposed to see through the loaned but rejected field glasses. He sees instead a donkey, a beast of burden. Later donkeys are reported to "bray to / each other, and turn in the fact of a simple circle." Eventually the poem circles back to the statement of the donkey's having come into the speaker's life at the moment he has taken from the box the loaned field glasses which would allow him to see stags on the mountain. The speaker's unstated question runs something like, "Why should I bother looking through field glasses for stags when a miraculous donkey has just come into my life?" The whole idea is humorous because we have the phrase (unspoken) "a woman / a man came into my life" running concurrent with the entrance of the donkey. Vision through the field glasses is a magnified vision of the miraculous being. The stag through the field glasses will lose the context of the mountain, his smallness in the wild. So the narrowing of vision, which allows closeness in one sense, estranges in another. The speaker proposes to lend the field glasses to "your stag" in a reversal of intended roles and a forcing of the stag image out upon the reader in the pronoun "your." The implication is that the reader should regard the speaker as an equally unapproachable creature, "the distant star." His smallness at the end of the poem suggests that the only way to truly know him is from the same distance a stag requires, not through field glasses, which artificially insist on a closeness that violates the very reason the stag was sought in the first place: its "strangeness" and "smallness."

One can't quite possess the knowledge of a wild animal seen from afar on a mountainside. It could be something else, a donkey, a tree stump, a "loan" of the imagination. So the poem is a rumination, a circling that suggests the way in which explications of texts intrude upon the wild intents of their makers—just as the formulation I have just made here is an intrusion, like putting field glasses on the donkey. It intrudes, is ridiculous, to the extent that it wants to fix the poem to one intent alone. There are many other implications and the reader is allowed to discover his own orientation to the narrative. The reader's responsibility here is not unlike that of spectators during the Renaissance when the creation of the vanishing point moved the spectator *into* the painting. This assumption of a space continuum between the painting and the spectator allowed the artist to get the spectator involved in the painting. "For the first time in the history of art, the *spectator shared the point of view of the artist.* A 'psychological vanishing point' was *created*" in the spectator.[12]

The "psychological vanishing points" of Burkard's poems are the intersections and unions of reflected meanings within the reader. Analyzed readings of the poems may bring the stag into eyeball-to-eyeball focus, but this is equivalent to head hunting or bird watching, in which one may congratulate oneself on having seen yet another "sociable lapwing." For this reason, I have chosen to devote most of this essay to

Burkard's method and his relationship to the reader rather than unraveling his poems for those who would wish to wring clarity from "a donkey on fire."

Burkard's poems remind us that the miraculous concerns those things we may not, cannot know or say. "Analysis operates always on the immobile, whilst intuition places itself *in* mobility" (Bergson). One must be agile and alive to the possibilities of words "on loan" to us and to themselves. This cannot be accomplished by standing outside the context of the poem like a stag with field glasses. One must use the naked eye, which causes stars, is fallible, and which, like memory, returns what it is able and makes up or loses the rest. Burkard's readers will be suitors, those chivalrous ones whose desire proceeds intuitively and for reasons as complicated as desire, or even as perverse. These suitors won't be out to secure a good housekeeper. They long for the ongoing pleasure of company that exceeds expectation, even when pleasure means learning to love as the love changes, as it must.

NOTES

My reading of the following sources extended over several years and during this time I did not know I would be writing an essay based on my notebook entries. Therefore, page numbers were not noted.

1. Gottfried Wilhelm Leibniz, quoted in *The State of the Language,* ed. Leonard Michaels and Christopher Ricks (Berkeley: University of California Press, 1980).

2. P. Adams Sitney, "The Cinematic Gaze of Joseph Cornell" in *Joseph Cornell,* ed. Kynaston McShine (New York: Museum of Modern Art, 1981). Hereafter cited in the text as Sitney.

3. Quoted in Edward Lucie-Smith, *Late Modern: The Visual Arts Since 1945* (New York: Oxford University Press, 1975). Hereafter cited in the text as Lucie-Smith.

4. Seamus Heaney, *Preoccupations: Selected Prose 1968–1978* (New York: Farrar Straus, 1980). Hereafter cited in the text as Heaney.

5. Henri Bergson, *An Introduction to Metaphysics,* trans. T. E. Hulme (New York: Bobbs-Merrill, 1949) (my italics). Hereafter cited in the text as Bergson.

6. All Michael Burkard poems are from *Ruby for Grief* (Pittsburgh: University of Pittsburgh Press, 1981).

7. Carl G. Jung, *Man and His Symbols* (New York: Doubleday, 1954). Hereafter cited in the text as Jung.

8. Anatole Broyard, "New Woman," *New York Times Book Review*, January 10, 1982 (my italics).

9. Roland Barthes, *The Pleasure of the Text*, trans. Richard Miller (New York: Hill and Wang, 1975). Hereafter cited in the text as Barthes.

10. J. T. Fraser, *Of Time, Passion, and Knowledge* (New York: George Braziller, 1975).

11. Gertrude Stein, quoted in *The State of the Language*, ed. Michaels and Ricks.

12. Marshall McLuhan, *Through the Vanishing Point—Space and Poetry and Painting* (New York: Harper and Row, 1968).

147

Like a Strange Guest of the Earth
The Poems of Linda Gregg

Poetry is something like religion in a wild state.

—Novalis

Just when the voices in the poetry we have been reading in America seemed to be cozy with digressions and dailiness, minimalist in their aims, rising to passion only when it was possible to carry irony safely, there appears a most unexpected voice, and doing what no one thought to do—finding reason to rejoice!

What is more, the pretexts for this rejoicing are not vested in any startling new dimension. They are the things we had all along: "wind and leaves mixing," "the creek with the small fish in it, / and the sounds of the sea at the edge of a field." Why then should the poems of Linda Gregg cause, as they do in me, a feeling of spiritual abundance? Why do they lift one cleanly and surely into an imagination which ignites all that surrounds it?

Always it is the journey to such arrivals which convinces, and even with poems that startled me when I met them on their own, such as "Whole and without Blessing" and "Blake," I acknowledge their power still more after rereading other poems in which the pain is given so acutely and with so little asking that the reader must look, as the speaker does, with a gaze that may not be turned away.

Keats tells us that the highest poetry will be written by "those to whom the miseries of the world / Are misery, and will not let them rest." What authenticates Gregg's work for me is that she does not flinch before actual or imagined horrors. She does not turn them into a sideshow for her own ego. One feels instead the steady struggle of a woman who wants to live in the world, but who at the same time needs a spirituality which demands purity to such a degree that she is often driven out of the human. The poems which witness and enact the struggle between the human and the nonhuman, between sensuality and purity of being are many, but I am thinking here of "There she Is," "Lilith," "This Place," "The Grub," "Eurydice," and "Marriage and Midsummer's Night."

It is perhaps her very openness to pain which makes the strength of this voice so considerable—not how she uses pain, but how she is used *by it*:

> I am not supposed
> to turn away. I am supposed to see each detail
> and all expression gone.

With all expression gone, she relinquishes blame or judgment and the experience is often approached with a strange equanimity. In "The Grub" we are told "even the rim is cooking him," and we watch the grub move "tentatively down the side of the frying pan until he touches the frying grease with his whole face." The illuminating phrase here is "but he is falling by definition," reminding us that falling is a word applied to a direction which has metaphorical implications apart from the actions of the grub, who seems to have sought out the frying grease.

We feel vulnerability as a power in "Whole and without Blessing":

> I belong to no one. I do not move.
> I do not need to move. I lie naked on a sheet
> and the indifferent sun warms me.
> I was bred for slaughter, like the other
> animals. To suffer exactly at the center,
> where there are no clues except pleasure.

The word "slaughter" comes down like a hatchet because the rest of the poem has been so poised. The speaker aligns herself with a hill earlier in the poem, but by introducing her kinship with animals she enforces the word slaughter more crucially and causes us to experience the suffering as mute, thereby amplifying it. That pleasure is the only clue to this suffering is paradoxical. It feels untrue or anyway contrary to how we're used to thinking of suffering. The pleasure feels connected to the sexual, the instinctual, to those acts of being which drag us along behind them through pleasure into suffering. Reading this passage aloud, the repeated "er" sounds make an offering even of the mouth. It is the word pleasure which lingers and plays back over the poem. The speaker seems magnificently self-sufficient, as though she has borrowed strength from what is least human in the landscape.

Gregg is continually reconstituting elements in the landscape and in herself, testing them to prove them more than they seem. Even light must be broken toward its wholeness in the sun:

> The light is crushed and flies up,
> back to the sun.
> Rejoice in the breaking of the light.
> Rejoice when you are two and one.

In a small poem where the speaker climbs the mountain, we see the steps in terms "of absence" and "things broken." The moon represents some primitive or divine power and the speaker wants "to see if the moon is a mouth. / To see if I am what it wants." Again, even if it means that the self will be devoured, it seems the speaker is prepared, is able for the offering.

There are so many poems of Gregg's which introduce this primitive power in mysterious ways that mention must be made of a few. I am thinking of "The Poet Goes About Her Business" with the snake at the close, "covered with dust" and knowing "exactly where it wanted to go. / Toward any dark trees." Also, in "The Gods Must Not Know Us," the ecstatic passage:

> The world gives forth beauty
> like the great glad women in the dream.
> It overwhelms us. Spills over.

> I am afraid the earth will take it back
> and part of myself will get lost
> and I will not be a fitting gift.

> The gods must not know us well or they would
> not dance so openly, so happily before us.

And in "We Manage Most When We Manage Small":

> The stars do not blow away as we do.
> The heavenly things ignite and freeze.

There are quieter poems infused with a mixture of pathos and joy, as in "Too Bright To See":

> Sweet being, if you are anywhere that hears,
> come quickly. I weep, face set, no tears, mouth open.

And also from "Not Singing":

> We sing of loss because the only voice they gave us
> was song and reasoning. It is not love we are after.
> No love. Not singing. But a somber thing.
> A going to the opening and entering.

Gregg's pacing in the poems is tacitly careful. Her emphasis is not on image-making, though she does this well, but on dramatic placement, noticing, cataloguing as though the consciousness might be overwhelmed by abundance or unreasonableness if it did not choose to locate itself and others within the landscape. It is this calculation in the movement of the lines which gives the poems their heroic tone, and not an elevation of diction as is more often the way of achieving the classical. Here the diction is kept simple, the manner lucid, with a childlike sensibleness that is capable of lyric bursts: "You who felt me turn / into the thousandth spirit with my name / in your hands."

The only contemporary poet whose tone similarly approaches the classical is Olga Broumas who, like Gregg, has lived in Greece. Her poem "Innocence" moves toward God through the sensuality of love for another woman. But for me, her approach stays in the ecstatically sensual as Gregg's does not, perhaps because Gregg's poems never assume that love is simply a good since it carries the possibility of loss. Since this loss is more than physical, the poem's energies are ultimately located in spiritual need. For instance, in "Not of Knowledge but of Expectation," there is the sense of the self having been consumed by a love about which there is no choice, so obsessive it goes on as an unquenchable longing after the loved one has left. Just as the reader thinks the speaker is going to head into blame, into accusation—"You who walked away with my life / leaving me with just enough to stay alive"—the claim is relinquished, "not that I mind." The loved one is then seen as one who pursues a mission which is as selfless as the elements: fire, rain, light. So the speaker acknowledges purposes beyond choice, for herself and the lover. Still, regret is expressed in the simple unearthing of a wall on Atlantis

> with the red lilies and swallows flying on it,
> and no people. It is the same with all
> which has been refined. Radiant. The same.

The lilies and swallows happen not as images but as actualities—*red* lilies and swallows *flying* so that they are at once animated and stilled on the wall. The "no people" forces the images back into stasis. They recede even further when the repeated phrase "the same" becomes the ending. It is an ending which flutters, flares with the isolated word *radiant* given as a full sentence. "The same" diminishes and holds this radiance. It refers back to the wall with its trapped yet animated lilies and swallows. These are seen as having been "refined"— refined in the sense that they exist beyond their creators, just as the unmentioned past of the lovers survives them, not only as knowledge but as expectation. The idea of flight is attached to a bird image on a wall, the thought that it might fly, though it doesn't. Similarly, there is the thought that their love continues, though it is held in the shape of that perceived moment which only expectation may free.

Expectation has a negative function in its prolongation of

desire after the loved one is gone. It is our expectations which often keep us from seeing the wholeness of things, what possibilities should be honored in a life. Expectation is also then the warp in the mirror, causing hurt because it leaps ahead of what *is*. In knowledge we see this, but in expectation we try to fix the future, to force the self and its needs upon events. The pain, then, is a sign of our mistake, that we have forgotten the holy nature of the other which is not to be made use of. Gregg does not step back but travels straight through the pain, seeking light and energy for the renewal of joy.

The self in Gregg's poems is continually cast out in its attempts to sustain itself in terms of an other. It remains the spectator of its own attempts in many poems, but in its estrangement it discovers new, essential truths about the nature of giving.

Early in "Not of Knowledge but of Expectation" the speaker begins to "make lists of the sacred" in an attempt to restore worth to her vision of the world:

> This time of year it is the stillness of trees,
> the ease of hawks, pink quince in grey mornings.
> But these mean nothing to you.
> They are ungivable because I know them alone.

The line, "They are ungivable because I know them alone," suggests that we can give only those things already known together with the other. This is an original recognition. Gregg has seen that, paradoxically, what enables giving is the sharing of experience, not the solitary self approaching the loved one with its basket of delectables. It is impossible to give fully what is experienced in one's aloneness because the very fact of one's aloneness conditions the perception of the phenomenon—"the stillness of trees, / the ease of hawks, pink quince in grey mornings."

Gregg presents her exclusions without rancor, often as simply as she gives night to the trees, to the river. In "Marriage and Midsummer's Night," the first line, "It has been a long time now," makes one feel that the event to be described has been carried in the memory for a long time into the "now," not simply that it was a long time *ago:*

It has been a long time now
since I stood in our dark room looking
across the court at my husband in her apartment.
Watched them make love.
She was perhaps more beautiful
from where I stood than to him.
I can say it now: She was like a vase
lit the way milky glass is lighted.
He looked more beautiful there
than I remember him the times
he entered my bed with the light behind.
It has been three years since I sat
at the open window, my legs over the edge
and the knife close like a discarded idea.
Looked up at the Danish night,
that pale, pale sky where the birds that fly
at dawn flew on those days all night long,
black with the light behind. They were caught
by their instincts, unable to end their flight.

The scene is one returned to obsessively as though the speaker
is forced to reencounter it until the imagination can construct a
medium which will release the pain. She presents her husband
and the woman to herself like beautiful objects one might hold
admiringly to the light. Her vantage point allows the light to act
upon their images, making them ironically more beautiful to
her even than to each other. The light behind both figures
throws them into darkness so they occur to her together as the
husband had often appeared to her alone, entering her bed
"with the light behind."

The final resolution of the pain is managed through the
lighting, which causes the husband and the woman to be iden-
tified with the birds "caught by their instincts, unable to end
their flight." What is marvelous here is that we realize the
speaker too is trapped in this instinct of flight. The back-
lighting of the images forces the birds out toward the reader
as though at the end they become suddenly three-dimen-
sional, carried by flight past their own willing. There is more
than exoneration in this image. It represents a cleansing and
relinquishes the painful occasion to forces which need no rec-
tification.

I think of Louise Bogan when I read an ending like this. She was often able to give the sense of some externally extended motion, as in "the lean hound's body arched against the snow." She also comes to mind as an example of how the classical tone was used in her generation. While it gives Bogan a somewhat imperious stance at times, in Gregg the self is always disarming as though it were in a state of preparation, of seeking. Bogan's tone derived from her reticence and elevated diction. It seems to hear itself as echo, as speech perfected, while Gregg's speech seems to carry some implicit humility. Although the manner is high, the reader has the experience of accompanying a mind actively encountering itself. This adds an unexpected intimacy to the heroic stance.

There has been some feeling that since the advent of feminism it has become difficult for women to write poems which clearly honor their love for a man. Men are more likely to be regarded as problems in poetry written by women. And even if this is where the energy starts, one sometimes wishes it could be accomplished with less obvious additional damage to the participants and the territory.

Gregg has her own moments of almost quizzical triumph, as in the ending of "Being With Men": "The wife grows strange, but one does not comfort her. / It might look like he is guilty of something." The "like" saves the speaker from direct accusation, but makes its point that comfort is withheld from the wife because it *would* imply that the husband is guilty. Gregg's argument is finally not with men, but her own obsessive reenactments of moments when her exclusion threatens to blot her out entirely. Although the men in her poems do not satisfy her need for inclusion, the pain and failure of her attempts seem not to embitter her in their direction; rather, she is urged past these loves toward an ultimate recognition of divinity in all things. She does not demean her male counterparts, though she gains considerable ground over them in understanding and generosity of spirit in poems like "Marriage and Midsummer's Night" and "Eurydice."

Recent changes in the lives of women have begun to require strenuous attitudinal shifts, and these have followed us into our art. For instance, it may be more difficult now if a woman wants to admit the need of a man's love. Although there is already a backlash against poems in which women feel obligated to talk about breast-feeding, relationships with other women, and the frustrations of making it on their own, this predisposition toward so-called feminine subjects still may blind us to poems which want to reenter territory we thought we had left behind. Linda Gregg's poems reinstate the search for the other, be it man, woman, or God, as an important adjunct to the discovery of self, how it approaches its wholeness. And this concerns women. And this concerns men. Often together.

This too was also something we were supposed to have outgrown, the need for a god or some purifying principle. You have to go back to Blake, Milton, Donne, Emily Dickinson, and Roethke if you want to hear poets talking to God. The search for the self apart from any divine principle has replaced the search for God since Nietzsche declared man self-sufficient. And as for Paradise, well we don't hear much energy in that direction either. Here again, Gregg manages to resurrect these concerns as though they had never left us. "If Paradise is to be here / it will have to include her," she says at the end of "There She Is." It is as though the speaker is also the maker, the consort, at least, of the god who goes into the garden to find a woman who has eaten her hands off. *If* Paradise is to be *here,* here in the garden? here on the earth? Not elsewhere, not in heaven, but *here.* What the poem brings us to realize is that Paradise must always be elsewhere when suffering like this is before one. The force of the ending is to "have to include her" so that Paradise *does* happen *here* and she *is* included, even in the mutilation of her own body out of extreme need. The image of the mutilation of the body recurs in Gregg's poems perhaps as representation of what the spirit is also undergoing, certain amputations and disfigurements. An unanswerable, superhuman dimension of pain is revealed in these poems, which turns the speaker toward wonder and horror, often at consequent moments, as in "The Chorus Speaks Her Words as She Dances," which begins

You are perishing like the old men. Already your arms are
    gone.

Your legs filled with scented straw tied off at the knees.
Your hair hacked off. How I wish I could take on each part
of you as it leaves. Sweet mouse princess. I would sing
like a nightingale, higher and higher to a screech
which the heart recognizes, which the helpless stars enjoy—
like the sound of the edge of grass.

I want to mention Galway Kinnell's *The Book of Nightmares*
as a rare example in contemporary poetry of the search for
the divine. In this book-long poem, with its retelling of the
birth moments in human and mythic terms, the relentless
musculature of language poured into the darkness, we have
worship, we have the arms still uplifted toward a god. And
though it is a primitive god that Kinnell approaches, the god
of sudden furies and equally sudden mercies, this feeling of
beings under a higher and mysterious power is made to live
again for us in the language.

Gregg's conception of the divine is rooted more in the
ancient tragic myths. There are gods, plural, as in one of her
titles, "The Gods Must Not Know Us." This plurality of gods
is authentic for Gregg because she has absorbed them imagi-
natively. Donne approached God as one might approach a
lover, wooing and cajoling. Gregg approaches God and the
gods as ultimate powers who may not find men and women
particularly significant in the whole range of creation. She
often assumes the role of the supplicant, preparing her mind,
her body, "Air moves around me and I prepare. / Make a gift
of myself. Make my feet soft." The old flags of tragedy begin
to fly again: courage and inevitable defeat, terror and pity
caught in equipoise in her poem "This Place":

> It makes me wonder why
> I saw lions as guardians, angels flexing their jaws,
> tightening against the walls for pity's sake.
> I cry out to them with my burned mouth
> full of joy and wonder: "Pity, I have found you."
> Pity, I bring you a present of my mind, complete
> with the sweet smell of the King's garden
> when you come into it from a small distance.
> I have not made you up. You are here.

She makes her place in this universe with her voice, her calling out to the emblems of the sacred, even those elements of the creation which seem formidable, like the guardian lions who "see me calling, and we move closer." This closeness may not be the closeness of the lion and the lamb who will eventually lie down together. She could as easily be devoured as pitied, and she knows this.

We are used to dismissing any experience which stresses pain by using the word *masochistic*. This word has done much damage because the truth is that suffering is still, whether we welcome it or not, perhaps at the heart of what we may know of ourselves and others. So, while the word *masochistic* has perhaps made us more "prudent," it has unfortunately discredited the genuine willingness of some rare spirits among us who have refused to turn back from the extremes of pain which seemed to them the necessary terms of their own journeys.

A poem that is especially vulnerable to this charge is Gregg's "They Think the Untouched Ones More Beautiful." The speaker in this poem is not deemed worthy or beautiful because she is one of the "touched" ones, those whom experience has bruised:

> They think the untouched ones more beautiful than me.
> But I love the worms
> eating and pushing through my baby fat.
> The dark, sweet feeling that my bruises hold
> mates me more than a lover.
> I am ravished in my revealed core.
> I set animals the scent
> and they writhe in my pleasure,
> eating bluntly at what I have left.

By the end of the poem the phrase, "what I have left," meaning what is left of me *and* what *I leave* to them though I am gone, causes a reversal in which the touched become the untouched. Her consciousness mates itself to the pain the worms cause as they push through, and she welcomes the eventual—that we will all be touched, that the worms will come—and the poem ends with the triumph of the eaten over the eaters. The consciousness raises itself out of the purely carnal in the line "I am ravished in my revealed core," though the image is perhaps so horrifying because it suggests a sexual wound as well. I am reminded of a line in *Justine* by Lawrence Durrell where Alexandria is described as "the great winepress of love" in which those who "emerged from it were the sick men, the solitaries, the prophets—I mean all those who have been deeply wounded in their sex." It seems appropriate that prophets and solitaries are given here in the company of sick men and those "wounded in their sex," which calls to mind Gregg's "Different Not Less."

Another such passage occurred for me near the start of *Justine,* a book imbued with the spirit of the ancient world, which gave me much experience of the landscape, light, and the intellectual and mythic dimensions of the life there. The narrator approaches the transformation of pain as necessary for the creation of art:

> Our common actions in reality are simply the sackcloth covering which hides the cloth-of-gold—the meaning of the pattern. For us artists there waits the joyous compromise through art with all that wounded or defeated us in daily life; in this way, not to evade destiny, as the ordinary people try to do, but to fulfill it in its true potential—the imagination. . . . In thought I achieve them (those who have been a part of my struggle) anew; as if only here—this wooden table over the sea under an olive tree, only here can I enrich them as they deserve . . . weaving them into the supple tissues of human memory. I want them to live again in the point where pain becomes art. . . .

Gregg's work throws into question for me at points another currently popular idea, that one should beware of giving up any substantial need for the sake of another, whether lover, husband, wife, child, or friend. "Personal growth" and "autonomy" are to be sought, whatever the cost, and while it is true that these are routes toward gain in some areas, it oversimplifies the way maps fail to include the view.

In "Different Not Less" we encounter the line, "Each gives over where its nature is essential." This, according to Gregg, is exactly the point at which any surrender or relinquishment of being *must* take place—at the most important mark of its difference.

> The river loses all but a sound.
> The bull keeps only its bulk.
> Some things lose everything.
> Colors are lost. And trees mostly.
> At a time like this we do not doubt our dreams.
> We believe the dead are standing along the other edge
> of the river, but do not go to meet them.
> Being no more powerful than they were before.

If trees, which are so special a phenomenon in the day, can be so overtaken, then what might not happen? There is the desire in this poem as in much of Gregg's work to make human wholeness match the wholeness of the universe. That is, if the natural world has an inherent order, then our discovery of that order may give perspective to what otherwise seems formless or arbitrary in our own lives. If Gregg had written "*Equal* Not Less" we would have missed the genius of this poem, which is its revelation of our difference while it brings the physical world toward us with its own difference intact. The "not less" is worked out invisibly as we accept our turn in the "coming around" of the pattern. We also allow these different worlds their boundaries:

> We believe the dead are standing along the other edge
> of the river, but do not go to meet them.
> Being no more powerful than they were before.

This last line invites more than one reading: no more powerful than the dead were before they died? and by implication, no more powerful than we? no more powerful than before we noticed them or than they have always been? All of these are possible.

> Modestly we pass our dead in the dark,
> and history—the Propylaea to the right
> and above our heads. The sun, bull-black
> and ready to return, holds back so the moon,
> delicate and sweet, may finish her progress.

I like how "modestly" and "our dead" balance each other so that it is belonging, not possession, we feel. The mention of history in proximity to "the Propylaea," or gates to the temples, seems to locate it as "above our heads," as though it too, like the night, waits to drop over us. The incorporation of the bull into the sun as "bull-black" combines the powers of the day with those of the night. There is a persuasion of goodness over all.

In the final lines, Gregg uses our acknowledgment of night's ascendancy early in the poem to lead us into equal trust that death and loss, "what is not given," is also a "world alive," though it is "another" and "our wholeness [is] finishing." Again, Gregg does not say "our part finishing," she says "our wholeness finishing," and we then ask: But how can a wholeness finish? We feel our own reluctance to "give over" where our nature is essential—in our living—yet the momentum of the argument and the action of the word "finishing" over "wholeness" forces us into the pattern.

When one of us actually enters into that difference of "another world" we are able to travel *with* our finishing, and also to look back on what we were. In two poems which signal a mythic relationship in their titles, "Eurydice" and "Lilith," we get this "outside looking back" view, although we are at the same time within the "outside" view.

What often causes poems patterned on myths to fail for me is that they are so conscientious in paying their respects to the myth, they trot along behind it, simply substituting a modern situation or language. There is some parallel pleasure in this and often much humor, but the myth too often overwhelms the writer's own experiences, causing a lack of dimension. Gregg's use of myth is rather as overlay on insistently private territory which takes resonance and situation from the title. Then she immediately plunges into her own urgencies. Still, there are some intended turnabouts on the myths which occur in both poems. In "Eurydice," Gregg's speaker tells the Orpheus of the poem who has come to lead her out of hell:

> You were always curious what love is like.
> Wanted to meet me, not bring me home.
> Now you whistle, putting together

the new words, learning the songs
to tell the others how far you traveled for me.
Singing of my desire to live.

Orpheus is seen not as the valiant husband who braves hell to
bring his wife back to earth, but as more concerned with how
he can use her pain and exile as artistic collateral for his own
songs, his glory. In the myth, Orpheus must lead Eurydice
out of hell without looking back, but he does look back and
she disappears. In Gregg's poem it is as if Orpheus never
intended to lead Eurydice out of hell. His looking back will
take the form of the songs, the memories and stories he gives
of her when he returns to earth alone. Even though she is
aware she will not be led out, she paints her eyes for the
journey, allows the Orpheus figure to take her "almost to the
world." It is "almost" not only because of the faithlessness of
her guide, but because in a sense she did not *want* to go back,
has found the way out of the world in looking back on it. In
this way she joins Orpheus in having traded life for memory.
Her tragic flaw, if you will, may be given in the lines:

Inside my mind and in my body is a darkness
which I am equal to, but my heart is not.

It is through a weakness of the passions, the desires, that
Gregg's speaker has experienced a loss of the world, a
"mourning." The heart is unequal to the continual loss it
would have to endure in the world. Orpheus, because he is
glibly oblivious to all this, comes off badly. It is intimated that
his incomplete perception of their love has contributed to
their separation:

Oh, if you knew what you do not know
I could be in the world remembering this.

At the close of the poem he goes back to a world which is no
longer the possible world for her, not the way in, but the way
out. In "Eurydice Saved" Gregg calls art "the imitation /
of what we called nothing when we lived on the earth." She
returns value to that "nothing," thereby saving herself, not by
going back to the world, but by using art to recover the im-

portance which the living could not acknowledge. Hell then has the legacy of art.

One of the consistent means of revelation in the poems is the creation of miniature dramas in which the speaker enacts her emotional and spiritual dilemma through some collaboration with the landscape. In the second part of "Lilith," Gregg uses stones as metaphor:

> I line up five stones on the ground.
> I count them. I laugh
> even though I am alone.
> Remembering how the men never knew
> how reasonable I am.

The stones represent the men who "found me and used me" and she enacts her freedom from them by damming the river, then releasing it to its natural flow.

> They are afraid of the pain
> they have given me. I made a dam
> in the creek today and then took
> the stones away.

Thus she aligns herself with nature. And if she does not accept her aloneness, at least she finds a way to order it among the other signs of God's presence.

In the original Jewish legends and in the Talmud, "Lilith" appears as the first wife of Adam. She was composed of the same dust and therefore refused to serve him and was said to have uttered the ineffable name of God and then flown away.

Gregg does not present a demon but a woman who has been exiled from human company to a woods. She looks back on her encounters with men as Eurydice looks back from hell to the earth. She seems reconciled to "dark trees, bright lights." She is in communion with the powerful elements of the landscape and walks each day to look at the ocean "at the edge of the world." This detail causes the ocean to extend infinitely as in the days before Pythagoras intuited that the earth was round and therefore contained. And she partakes of this infinity.

In the third section she presents herself as double, more

openly than she has in the Alma sequence, where a part of the self splits off and is, in many cases, "done to" rather than a participant. This double seems capable of self-compassion but the speaker sends her away, unable to accept kindness even though "never has there been more agreement / between anyone." She goes on acting out the pain, falling down, "crying for anything but woman to ease my suffering." The word "for" is ambiguous for me here. Does she mean she wants *only* woman or anyone *but* woman? She seems to say even death would be more kind than having to accept comfort from her own kind. Perhaps if this is a mirror likeness, it is also quite frightening to see one's own image magnifying the loss already felt inside:

> I open the door.
> She is standing there with tears on her face,
> just like before. Unsure whether to start again.

What is to start again, one wonders? The return to the world which has "made use" of her? The weeping? The whole drama of interior pain made external? It is the shutting of the door before it is opened which is an ingenious touch. It makes us feel that the woman will never go away, just because she has stood through this refusal. She calls to mind Niobe, the woman of sorrow in the Bible. The meeting enacts the speaker's need to participate in her own estrangement, as if she were the god of herself working toward the extension of pity to herself.

As the poem ends, we enter the ruined Paradise where Lilith walks "through the fields of rotting bodies" to get a bucket of water. She brings to mind the Egyptian goddess Isis, who stood with one foot on land and one on water, and she takes on more of the mediating aspect of the feminine "principle." A medieval mystical text which Jung has quoted from presents this figure in terms which make her familiar to my discussion of Gregg's work thus far:

> That which is dry I make moist and the reverse, and that which is hard I soften. . . . I am the law in the priest and the word in the prophet. . . . I will kill and I will make live and there is none that can deliver out of my hand.

The battlefield "end" in "Lilith" seems to have been sig-
naled by a false adoration of women in which "statuary used
to fill the gardens of rich and powerful men." After this, the
wars. Lilith seems fortunate to have withdrawn from such
men. Now she looks toward a time when what might be called
"the feminine principle" will reenter the pattern:

> Gradually there will be gardens again.
> First for food and then also for flowers.

Her own exile is a part of this pattern, and the idea that
gardens and the raising of food and eventually flowers will
return indicates that her own exile may also be ending.

No mention is made of Lilith's defiant nature as one who
refuses to serve men with whom she is equal. Feminist poetry
has already given enough on this aspect of the myth. Gregg
chooses to redeem Lilith not by righteous anger, but by her
own resourcefulness. She finds other ways of sustaining her-
self than through the needs of men. But she does not flaunt
this strength and it seems all the more sure for that restraint.

In the "Blake" poem the essence of Blake seems likewise to
have been absorbed personally. He is not a personage but is
omnipresent as light, as sun on the roof. This poem soars so
high in its celebratory wholeness that it is hard to know how
one would go on from this—as though this translucence of
spiritual ecstasy had gained not only the mountain top, but
the mountain. Gregg's inner strategies for arriving at speech
for these experiences are so particular to her turn of mind
and spirit that she is unlikely to have many imitators. She will
not provide other poets with a way of speaking into their
experience from which they may stylistically borrow, as poets
like Ashbery and Olson and Merwin to some extent have
done. Rather her value is that she challenges the consequence
of a large field of contemporary writers who have perhaps
aimed too low and who now may be encouraged to define
their own visions as substantially as Gregg has.

When I look further in Gregg's work for the kind of energy
which is going to sustain and nourish this new voice, I find it in
poems which question systems of belief that suggest we must
retreat from life in order to ensure perfection. Gregg insists

that our lives and art be acted out in nothing less than ultimate perspectives. In a new poem, "What If the World Stays Always Far Off," she has begun to move into the world, to include figures other than husbands, lovers, doubles. She is in the world of bosses and workers, a world in which she participates:

> Nobody talks to the Jamaicans. They are driven
> to Safeway in the bus and brought back.
> I saw one alone just standing by the woods.
> "I send money to my mother if I feel like it,"
> he said to impress me. About eighteen.
> He will cut cane for the first time this year.
> "I hear the bosses are mean," I said.
> "We make more money," he said. "It is a longer time."

"Gnostics on Trial" draws the battle lines, puts on trial the ascetic view that those who live least, who create no debris in the fervor of their journey toward perfecting their lives, are those who will inherit the Kingdom of God. As the poem demonstrates, it is the very abundance of the world which refutes the gnostic mandate to limit one's happiness in an unhappy world:

> Disregard that afternoon breeze from the Aegean
> on a body almost asleep in the shuttered room.
> Ignore melons, and talking with friends.

Gregg closes with a challenge we may use in its full generosity:

> Try to keep from rejoicing. Try
> to keep from happiness. Just try.

Throwing the Scarecrows
from the Garden
The Poetry of Marianne Moore

In 1970 when I began to read Marianne Moore in a class with the poet Jean Garrigue, I was determined not to like Moore's poems. But they were on the menu and I allowed my nose to be pressed into the plate—not by Ms. Garrigue, who was the gentlest of teachers, but by the poems themselves. I resented what I took to be their holier-than-thou, near Olympian chill, the lack of visible emotion, the magpie clutter, the pert glint in the bird's eye that said I was too dull-witted to ever catch her meaning without a sojourn in the moat. Luckily, this was not to be the lasting impression Moore made on me.

I happened upon George Eliot's insistence that "women have not to prove that they can be emotional and rhapsodic, and spiritualistic; everyone believes that already. They have to prove that they are capable of accurate thought, severe study, and continuous self-command."[1] It was a call for women to "rebut the generalizations which had encouraged their onesidedness."[2] Looking at Moore's work in this light, I quickly began to revise my attitude toward her poetry and developed a hard-earned advocacy by the end of the course.

I begin here with my failure toward her work because I believe it to be the rule with readers, having by now taught her to classes myself—classes populated with recalcitrant Moore-haters, some of whom are never converted. One aspect of general reluctance toward her work arises from a too-narrow definition of passion, which young people especially yearn for in poetry. Being so vested in bodily notions in our

167

first understanding of the word passion, we neglect what Louise Bogan called "a passion wholly of the mind." It is here that Moore's poetry is situated.

Such misunderstanding of Moore is not restricted to the young or the uninitiated. In her book, *Naked and Fiery Forms: Modern American Poetry by Women: A New Tradition,*[3] the critic Suzanne Juhasz continues a tradition of using Emily Dickinson to beat Moore over the head, Moore being "without Emily Dickinson's range and passion."[4]

If passion is the capacity to show evidence of burning, of being carried by one's enthusiasms and frustrations, then Moore has it. Time and time again we see her expertly adrift on her own tides, especially in the long poems such as "An Octopus" and "Marriage." When Moore gives us "the roar of ice" in "An Octopus"[5] I find myself thinking that this is indeed the cumulative effect of this poem, which begins in the seeming desolation "of ice. Deceptively reserved, and flat" and ends "in a curtain of powdered snow launched like a waterfall." Her intensity is analogous to "the unegoistic action of the glaciers." Line by line Moore populates the mountain like Noah's ark turned upside down. On it are "bears, elk, deer, wolves, goats and ducks" as well as a water ouzel and a marmot. She is attentive also to the flora of the mountain:

> birch-trees, ferns, and lily-pads,
> avalanche lilies, Indian paint-brushes,
> bear's ears and kittentails,
> and miniature cavalcades of chlorophylless fungi

With the "relentless accuracy" which is the passion of the naturalist and the scientist and of this artist, she observes the mountain and also what the mountain is not. It is not where some of these animals have their dens; they come there for things they need, just as the reader visits the worlds writers provide in order to experience joys and hardships of habitats other than those to which they have become accustomed. Moore's tertiary movement in the poem allows her to intend a direction and then turn back on it; or, she will embellish a minor movement until it takes on noteworthy proportions and has to be considered a legitimate digression relevant to some compelling inner sense of appropriateness she feels toward the subject. What emerges is a dialogue concerning interiors and surfaces. At first, one begins to feel that the mountain *is* what is *on* it. But as the poem nears its conclusion we are brought to understand that the ultimate forces of the mountain, as with Moore's writing, are unseen, "creeping slowly as with meditated stealth." It is not the surface which has the last say here, but the interiors which have been "planed by ice and polished by wind," and which have the power to send avalanches "with a sound like the crack of a rifle."

Juhasz seems unaware that the definition of passion also admits "appetite" and is synonymous with fervor, enthusiasm, zeal, and ardor; all "denoting strong feeling, either sustained or passing, for or about something or somebody. Enthusiasm as it relates to passion "reflects excitement and responsiveness to more specific or concrete things."[6] It is in her enthusiasm and responsiveness that we must locate Moore's passion, and if she loves "in a mild distant, sisterly way"[7] it is still loving, and a variety of loving perhaps much underrated when opposed to the Latin sense of self-abandonment, which argues for an authenticity based on surrender of the will. It is Moore's insistence on maintaining the means and terms of her loving, her responsiveness, that we should admire as something progressive in the literature of women.

To get closer to Moore's sense of passion, one must read her essay on Pavlova, in which she notes that the Russian dancer was "self-controlled rather than a prison to what she prized," that "she did not project as valuable the personality from which she could not escape," and finally, that "that which is able to change the heart proves itself."[8] Each of these insights may be valuably applied to Moore's own attitudes toward her art.

One cannot miss Moore's love for what this woman communicated of the human spirit by way of what Moore saw as the most naked of the arts—dance. The connection to Pavlova is so deep that Moore cannot resist retelling the circumstances of Pavlova's death in the chronology she provides at the end, so that the piece concludes with Moore's own sense of the loss of this beautiful, passionate presence:

> In January 1931 she died in Holland, of pleurisy. While enroute to the Hague via the Rivera, to begin a tour, after a sleepless night in a train that had stood on a siding all night, she caught cold—recorded thus reverently by Mr. Beaumont: "Hardly settled in the Hotel des Indes, she fell ill; the flame that was her life flickered, burnt low, and half an hour after midnight, on Friday, January 23rd, went out."[9]

Moore did not need to supply this ending in such detail. The first line of this passage would have sufficed. The loss of the flame, the very metaphor Moore chooses to repeat in Mr. Beaumont's description, was necessary to what Moore needed to communicate of her own sense of Pavlova's intensity—her fire. One can't be a bystander to passion when it arrives so artfully given. Yet Moore appreciated in Pavlova the way in which her passion separated her even from those with whom she danced: "for in her dancing with persons, remoteness marked her every attitude."[10] This might also be applied to the remoteness of Moore's own tone in her poems at times.

I smile to think of Moore "sitting in" on Louise Bogan's 1956 class at the YW-YMHA and being advised with the rest of the class to "keep your abstract thought for the prose, your emotions for the poetry," and to remember that "emotion should remain direct and uncomplicated . . . issuing from the heart, not the 'ego.' "[11] Moore was only partially obedient, ignoring the edict on abstractions and adopting directness in tone, while preferring to complicate her stance by recessing emotion or exchanging it for industry and insight. Emotion with her was itself form. And, of course, she must have decided all this long before her encounter with Bogan. It is this lack of visible emotion, what in speaking of Dryden and later of Auden has been called "the middle way" of writing, that has obscured Moore's particular brand of passion, for she reinterpreted the "middle" style to mean "the circumspectly audacious."[12] We are unused to meeting passion unattended by displays of emotion, except perhaps in its sharper forms, as with Swift or Pope.

The charge that Moore sacrificed emotion in order to be "one of the boys" is one I find particularly obtuse. But Juhasz adopts it and seems to imply some Uncle Tomism regarding an essential element of the feminine: that women are emotional beings and that emotion has to be in the work of women writers we admire as such. Oh hogwash! And give that woman a bucket of newts. This is exactly the kind of nonthinking that cripples our response to what is truly individual in the best writing of women. Feminist scripts, like all scripts, are anathema. I daresay that had Moore begun writing at the time I did, in the late sixties, she would have secured her poetry against the Belfast of feminist ideology in favor of some less compulsory relationship to feminist attitudes and its legitimate urgencies.

All one needs is a month-long stay in Northern Ireland to understand that all defections are not simply cowardice, as Juhasz implies when she notes that Moore abjures emotion. Good sense is often involved. Like Seamus Heaney leaving Belfast for Blackrock in the Republic of Ireland, Moore was capable of a stringent vigilance toward her gift. Since hers was a gift vested in the desire to deliver us from our biases rather than confirm us in them, she was especially wary of responses dominated primarily by the emotions. Her brand of morality was marked by its utter lack of evangelism. Perhaps this continues to delay her reception by some readers.

Another complaint of feminist critics seems to be that Moore is too obsequious, always sitting in the corner eating humble pie. In a time when women writers want to be seen as having fully assumed the powers of their craft through the authority of their own skills, Moore's insistence on humility at every turn must strike them as a reprimand and also as an obsolete pretense meant to throw the hounds off the scent of what they assume to be her self-satisfied withdrawal from responsible connection to her creations. This, however, is not at all her circumstance, but one conferred on her by our times.

For Moore, humility was connected to a genuine sense of Grace, of being allowed knowledge in the face of odds, of being allowed her very art, which had sources other than the audacity of her will. Or as Auden put it, "suffering plays a greater part than knowledge" in our acts of the will, and "one must not discount Grace."[13] Like Pavlova, Moore would have considered genius as a trust, "concerning which vanity would be impossible."[14] Humility was a form of honesty with Moore, an honesty which, Donald Hall has been shrewd enough to point out, was not in the least self-effacing. It is not a concession when one considers oneself to be a beneficiary, especially for an intellect like Moore's which, as she well knew, was fully prepared for what Grace would deliver. She did her share of the work and took requisite pride in that.

Reticence is another detraction Juhasz enlists against Moore. It is true Moore is often reticent, but in all the skillful, interesting ways. Take, for instance, Moore's agility at chain-linking quotations one with another from borrowed sources, and coupling them with her own observations until she can project them into a quite unanticipated structure having its own integrity . . .

> But someone in New
> England has known enough to say
> that the student is patience personified,
>   a variety
> of hero, "patient
>   of neglect and of reproach,"—who can "hold by
>
> himself." You can't beat hens to
> make them lay. Wolf's wool is the best of wool,
> but it cannot be sheared, because
> the wolf will not comply. With knowledge as
>   with wolves' surliness,
> the student studies
>   voluntarily, refusing to be less
>
> than individual. He
> "gives his opinion and then rests upon it;"
>   ("The Student," 101–2)

Or in "The Monkey Puzzle":

> this "Paduan cat with lizard," this "tiger in a bamboo
>   thicket."

"An interwoven somewhat," it will not come out.
....
It knows that if a nomad may have dignity,
Gibraltar has had more—
that "it is better to be lonely than unhappy."

Juhasz takes Moore's constant quoting of others as the sign of her unwillingness to accept responsibility for her own assertions. I prefer to see quotation as proof of Moore's ambition not to write simply in the isolation of the ego, but to write as if she were a team, or an orchestra:

> When three players on a side play three positions
> and modify conditions,
>   the massive run need not be everything.
>   ("Baseball and Writing")

She was willing to take responsibility to a new, enlarged arena then, to present and credit views other than her own, and to provide a context for hearing a concert of voices. She was, of course, the ever-present conductor. She chose the score, was enigmatically "galvanized against inertia," delivered her baton strokes beginning "far back of the beat, so that you don't see when the beat comes. To have started such a long distance ahead makes it possible to be exact. Whereas you can't be exact by being restrained."[15] She preferred the responsibility of conversation to the responsibility of the orator. Her allegiance was to community and individual at once, no small commitment, and she ironically recognized the ways in which one compromised the other in the ending to "Marriage" when she puts a quote within a quote, and writes " 'Liberty and union / now and forever'; / the Book on the writing-table; / the hand in the breast-pocket" (70).

Moore's homage to her sources, what she called her "borrowed" and "hybrid method of composition," was proof, I believe, of a generosity of spirit, which admitted that the work of the artist is often the result of "gifting" from others, as much as it is a matter of being gifted. It is an innovation not even Whitman, with all his pride of inclusion, thought to design.

One has only to read Moore's notes to the poems to be reminded of how rich nonliterary sources can be for a writer. Moore knocked down the fence around literature. She let in the writers of books about tigers, books on physiography and anthropology. The list includes the *Harvard Journal of Asiatic Studies*, the *New York Times*, the *I-Ching*, a tour book guide to Italy, a progress report from research on cancer, an article on "Plastic Sponge Implants in Surgery," the dictionary, the *Christian Science Monitor*, and even a letter from a curator of reptiles and amphibians.

Reading Moore in 1970, I was impressed with the voracity of her interests. Reading her again fifteen years later, I feel that somehow the diversity and particularity of the history, the geography, the flora and fauna, and the creatures of the earth have been regrettably neglected by today's poets. It is refreshing to read a poet who has bothered to find out about more than her own traumas.

It is the lack of the contemporary central and exposed "I" which allows Moore to generalize and to extend both the range of her subject matter and the moral import of her explorations. There seems to be something in the very nature of her moralist's approach which prohibits confession. Probably this comes from the need to speak from a position of relative immunity. Auden managed it with the public "we." Recently Frank Bidart in his dramatic narrative, *The War of Vaslav Nijinsky*, calls on Nijinsky to fight the battles of his moral questionings. The dismay as to how to classify Bidart's work is not unlike that accorded Moore's poems when they first appeared: should we call this poetry? Donald Hall has responded in Bidart's favor by enlisting Moore's reliance on "the genuine": "Bidart is not a confessional poet; he is dramatic and universal, a moral observer of humanity. . . . When I read poems that are 'not poetry,' and yet 'wholly genuine,' I know that I am in the presence of something new."[16]

While Bidart's newness rests in his dramatic stance, his mixing of prose passages with lyrical bursts and dialogue, Moore's newness in technical matters comes from her incorporation of actual bits of prose into the bloodstream of her lines. In this she presaged Ashbery's experiments with prose elements in diction and gesture, as well as perhaps the current borrowing from prose, which is characterized by a preference for methods of accumulating energy through narratives that comment upon one another, such as Robert Hass's "Pascal Lamb."[17]

No one, however, has shown signs of developing a moral equivalent to Moore's content. Her poems "have a sense of civilization about them"[18] that seems outside the grasp of contemporary American practitioners. Just as America now buys its cars, blenders, galoshes, and pharmaceutical supplies abroad, it also seems to be looking to the Irish, the Polish, the Turkish, and the Russians of Akhmatova's generation for spiritual and moral qualities. Here also deficits accrue, and only intermittently, firefly style, do single accomplished poems with a moral approach hint at the general lack of Made-in-America resourcefulness Moore so much exemplified in this respect. Moore's conclusion to her essay on Louise Bogan allows one to see the lack of illusion with which she faced such issues: "We are told, if we do wrong that grace may abound, it does not abound. We need not be told that life is never going to be free from trouble and that there are no substitutes for the dead; but it is a fact as well as a mystery that handicap is proficiency, weakness is power, that the scar is a credential, that indignation is no adversary for gratitude or heroism for joy. These are medicines."[19] She had, in other words, no miracle cures, and would have agreed with the anthropologist studying tribal healing who said, "spells are not communiques: they are gestures."[20]

Still, the mania for solutions is a pressure the artist is usually aware of and must with agility renounce. Doris Lessing on a recent tour in Australia remarked in a newspaper interview that she was appalled by the number of people in her audiences who asked her for answers to a set of wide-ranging problems that ran the gamut from personal to political to ideological and religious. What frightened her was the feeling that these people were hungry for answers, not hungry for ways of thinking toward the problems. They wanted to be told what to do, and this, as she realized, is very dangerous, because it signals that people's resources and patience for self-generated action and for defining alternatives are lamentably low. Dangerous also because it invites someone of perhaps not altogether unimpeachable motives to do just what is asked, to tell them what to do. And therein lies an end to freedom.

A similar trend plagues us in the public moralism of the Reagan era, which operates without (yes, surprise!) morality. Public moralism in any era seeks to substitute dogma and adman hype for authentic action and discovery. Moore's aesthetic scorns such remedies, although the rather Confucian style of the wisdom she often provided at the ends of her poems would at first seem to indicate the opposite. But cut your teeth on advice like:

> It was enough; it is enough
> if present faith mend partial proof.
>
> ("Enough," 187)

The application is in no one's hands but the reader's. Or, take the ending of "Elephants" in which Moore tells us that

> as Socrates,
>
> prudently testing the suspicious thing, knew
> the wisest is he who's not sure that he knows.
> Who rides on a tiger can never dismount;
>
> ("The Elephants," 130)

Here Moore has it both ways, saying wisdom depends on a certain unsureness toward "the suspicious thing," and yet presenting what seems a verity, that he "who rides on a tiger can never dismount." I mean, I wouldn't. It is this mixture of fable with aphoristic surety added to "conversities" that cause one not to know from moment to moment on which side the gavel is going to come down. *Conversities* is a word Moore invented to indicate that her meaning might work positively and negatively without canceling out either possibility. I can remember a wonderful afternoon in a café in my hometown during which Michael Burkard and I took a close look at "Critics and Connoisseurs." Whose side is she on? we kept asking. The ledger would strangely balance itself at moments when we seemed about to identify a victim. I don't think we ever did settle it. This "conscientious inconsistency," as she termed memory in "The Mind Is an Enchanted Thing," is active throughout her poetry as a guarantee against rigidity of vision and narrow mandates. As Moore said when speaking of Williams, "the truth of poetry is not dogma, but a cry of a whole soul." This does not mean Moore is reticent about what she values or the need for values. In "Values in Use" she makes clear that values should not overwhelm the use we make of them: "Certainly the means must not defeat the end" (181).

The tyranny of prescribed morality I spoke of earlier strikes me as not far removed from the feminist critic's practice of composing hit lists by ransacking a poet's work for poems useful to the cause, and if the tally is insubstantial, sending the writer to the purgatory of "unrecommended reading." Juhasz, for instance, found that "Marriage" was the only poem of Moore's that could be counted as clearly having feminine experience as a central subject. Evidently, lines such as "Marriage, tobacco, and slavery, / initiated liberty ("Enough," 186) were inadmissible. Nor did she note the application of sexual identity to a hedgehog in "His Shield" (144), which directs it somewhat pointedly, as Moore does in other animal poems in which she assigns the animal a sex.

> In his
> unconquerable country of unpompous gusto,
> gold was so common none considered it; greed
> and flattery were unknown.

In presenting the hedgehog as masculine here, Moore seems to highlight the pomposity men have for exactly these negative capabilities. Juhasz failed to surmise that Moore's femininity is most active in her tendency toward dualism, odd partnerships, and hairline distinctions between neighboring qualities or properties. Here I'm thinking of poems like "Granite and Steel" and "Voracities and Verities Sometimes Are Interacting," although there are many other poems I might have chosen to mention. Oppositions of themselves invite "our metaphorical thinking to make one the masculine and one the feminine counterpart."[21] But surely we needn't go to these extremes to accept the gifts of one who is our own.

If pressed, however, I would recommend that "Love in America," with its "benign dementia," its "a Midas of tenderness . . . nothing else," and its hiss of yesses at the end, be added to the stockpile of poems of particular interest to women. I would also single out " 'He Wrote the History Book' " for how it reminds us of the *male* signature over all history writing and the "you" of the feminine contribution "to your father's / legibility," which causes women to appear "sufficiently / synthetic." She ends the poem with a real karate chop disguised as a bouquet: "Thank you for showing me / your father's autograph." Some of Moore's animal poems also allow us humor toward feminine predicaments, sexual and not—my favorite of these being "The Lion in Love," with its: "Lions or such as were attracted / to young girls, sought an alliance," and "Love, ah Love, when your slipknot's drawn, / One can but say, 'Farewell, good sense' " (246, 247).

What is one to make of Juhasz's charge that in her work Moore separated "woman" and "poet" as the most effective means of achieving professional success"? Or that Moore concentrated upon "technical brilliance coupled with a marked exclusion of feminine experience from art"?[22] Reading this makes me feel I've been caught in a strange time warp in which it is suddenly revealed that Bach is inferior because he doesn't seem to know anything about reggae.

What is Moore writing about, then, if she is intent on neglecting feminine experience in order to make a success of herself? She is writing about aesthetic choices of all kinds, about being human in a world also inhabited by animals and insects whose territory we have largely colonized, which in the worst sense of colonial, as Moore points out, has never been synonymous with mercy. She veritably puts the human family back on Noah's ark, where we have to lie down with each other while the waters rise. Indeed, her focus is on our very *beingness* itself. The questions she's asking are every bit as important to me as what I might be interested in writing with a view to women's issues, although that does interest me.

Some of these questions are: What relation does the past have to the present? How do beauty and sensibility coexist when faced with an uncompromising power? How do we value, and why, and what? Is there such a thing as "progress" when we consider military endeavors ("fighting fighting fighting that where / there was death there may / be life" ["In Distrust of Merits," 137])? What is liberty? Union? How does one preserve judgment in a world of hucksters and "snake-charming controversialists" ("The Labors of Hercules," 53)? What is a critic's job? What is poetry and why should we value it? What endures? How do we choose? What is transcendence? Consolation? Envy? Charity? Justice? ("And so, as you are weak or are invincible / the court says white is black or that black crimes are white.")[23] How should one deal with an enemy? ("Choose wisdom, even in an enemy" ["The Bear and the Garden-Lover," 257].) What is freedom? ("The Power of relinquishing what one would keep" ["His Shield," 144]).

If this reads like Topic Time at the back of a high school civics text, Moore's handling of these questions is always more an approach than a tourniquet. She is a poet who needs the constellation *and* the morning star, though she might object to their being yoked by that despised connective *and*.

Moore, it seems likely, as with so many extraordinary women of her time, never assumed accepted sexual exclusions within the artistic, social, or political sphere, and so, in many ways, never had to confront such issues in the way contemporary women have had to, sexual imperatives having defined our intellectual, social, and psychological battlefields for the past fifteen to twenty years.

I confess to being weary of feminist honor rolls in which Moore is addressed condescendingly as if she were merely the crumpled first step toward the Acropolis of Plath. Moore is no carriage-drawn supplicant at the mercy of General Motors. She was an originator, not simply an entrepreneur. And if she was a spare-parts wizard, she knew how to make things work, and did. She was also no pussycat, as many like to infer from her "mousing pose" ("Style," 169). As she observed, "an animal with claws should have opportunity to use them ("Peter," 44), and she took several. How would you like, for instance, to have been the one for whom "The Steam Roller" was intended? Or told that you "lack half-wit"? Or that you are one of those "self-wrought Midases of brains / whose fourteen-carat ignorance aspires to rise in value" ("The Labors of Hercules," 53)? Nonetheless, Moore is closer to Molière than to Swift. She recognized Molière as a relative, I think, and paid homage to him in "To the Peacock of France," seemingly enjoying kinship in his lack of popularity in certain quarters. Like Molière, she was concerned with manners, with those discrepancies between civility and brutality, action and word, intention and outcome that make us smile and wonder at human nature, make us take up our cudgels or our shields. She was a true archaeologist of the spirit, curious and exacting before the remnant of some variegated attitude, or "the deft white-stockinged dance in thick-soled shoes!" ("A Carriage from Sweden," 132), the "mantle lined with stars" ("Spenser's Ireland," 112).

One last scarecrow I would like to fling from Moore's imaginary garden is the idea that because she was a spinster her poetry is marred by the limitations of that social role, as Roy Harvey Pearce has implied.[24] Juhasz goes even further by accusing Moore of "opting for nonsexuality" and thereby escaping "those feminine characteristics that threaten." Juhasz is ready to assign Moore to a museum by virtue of her chastity. "Chastity is non-engagement; it leaves one in a position of safety."[25] Chastity was not "a position of safety" then, nor do I suspect it to be now, and the correctness of chastity as metaphor must, I think, bear witness to the act in order to support itself. Moore, as she put it best herself, simply "was not matrimonially ambitious."[26] She was nobody's fool and must, like Emily Dickinson, have understood that to take a husband in those times was tantamount to signing one's artistic death warrant. Adrienne Rich has retrieved Emily Dickinson from the myth of the madwoman in the attic by pointing out that Dickinson had reasons for choosing solitude—she was at work! Moore chose the companionship and nurturing of her mother for not dissimilar reasons, I think. Certainly, had she been "inclined," she could have managed to marry. All this is beside the point. I'm interested in Moore precisely for her difference. If one has access to the ultimate in virgin thought, one ought to prize it, pay attention, not pronounce it remedial. Give me a smart woman any day, whatever her gynecological qualifications.

There are so many things Moore has given me as a writer and human being over the years that I feel I ought to have acknowledged them long before now. I've needed her distrust of easy answers, her wonderful humor—"Humor saves a few steps, it saves years" ("The Pangolin," 119). Her team spirit appeals to me, though I don't know much about baseball and I'd make a rotten cheerleader. But, I agree that some things have to be done together and that each person in that "together" has an important contribution. Still, I don't want to march or hear the national anthem played three times a day. And neither does Moore. I prize Moore's cinematic eye, the way she uses the close-up metaphor so you can forget what you saw and keep seeing: "the lion's ferocious chrysanthemum head," "the swan's maple leaflike feet." Her poems operate the way our sight does on objects at a distance, requiring us to guess what we're seeing before we can confirm it. There she is, like the retina, collecting until the image identifies itself as something seen for the first time. I enjoy how Moore often delays confirmation syntactically so that conclusiveness itself is mocked.

Moore's propensity for miniature self-portraits is rather like those childhood visual puzzles where one attempts to see how many faces are camouflaged in the seemingly unpopulated landscape of the drawing. She is always there in multiples, "porcupine-quilled": in her "complicated starkness" ("The Monkey Puzzle," 80), or as "that spectacular and nimble animal the fish, / whose scales turn aside the sun's sword by their polish" ("An Egyptian Pulled Glass Bottle in the Shape of a Fish," 83), or "an obedient chameleon in fifty shades of mauve and amethyst" ("People's Surroundings," 56), or "like electricity, / depopulating areas that boast of their remoteness" ("The Labors of Hercules," 53).

There was the trick of writing messages invisibly in lemon juice which I used once or twice as a child. The scarcity of matches made it impractical. But when you could manage to scorch the paper just right, it was a thrill to see the words appear on the page as if out of nowhere. This somehow describes the way Moore's poems affect me. If she tells me "Titles are chaff" ("'He Wrote the History Book,'" 89), I get out my matches to see what else might be on the page. Sure enough, the meaning-after-the-meaning ripples across the brain. I see she meant more than that titles are to be discarded. It's the chaff, after all, that protects the germ of the wheat until it's matured toward harvest. I blow out the match.

Some final advice to those about to encounter the newest wave of resistance to Moore's poetry: to drink from a waterfall you have to get wet, but don't stand under it.

On my first visit to New York City in the summer of 1971, Jean Garrigue had invited me to meet Marianne Moore. The car I was driving across the country from Washington State had a sieve for a radiator, and I did not arrive in time. In the meanwhile, Moore had become very ill. That February she died. I was grateful, in a way, not to have met her at that time. How do you say goodbye to a waterfall?

NOTES

1. George Eliot, "Women in France: Madame de Sable," in *Essays of George Eliot*, ed. Thomas Pinney (New York: Routledge and Kegan Paul, 1963), 53.

2. Lynne Sukenick, "On Woman and Fiction," in *The Authority of Experience: Essays in Feminist Criticism*, ed. Arlyn Diamond and Lee R. Edwards (Amherst: University of Massachusetts Press, 1977), 33.

3. Suzanne Juhasz, *Naked and Fiery Forms: Modern American Poetry by Women: A New Tradition* (New York: Harper and Row, 1976).

4. Roy Harvey Pearce, quoted in Juhasz, *Naked and Fiery Forms*.

5. Marianne Moore, "The Octopus," *The Complete Poems of Marianne Moore* (New York: Macmillan/Viking, 1982), 71–76. All further references to Moore's poetry are from *The Complete Poems* and appear in the text.

6. *The American Heritage Dictionary*, 2d ed. (Boston: Houghton, Mifflin, 1982).

7. Louise Bogan, writing to Morton Zabel about her affection for T. S. Eliot, whom she had just met. Quoted in Elizabeth Frank, *Louise Bogan: A Portrait* (New York: Knopf, 1985), 343.

8. Marianne Moore, "Anna Pavlova," in *Predilections* (New York: Viking, 1955), 147–60.

9. Moore, *Predilections*, 160.

10. Moore, *Predilections*, 160.

11. Frank, *Louise Bogan*, 346.

12. Frank, *Louise Bogan*, 85.

13. Moore, "W. H. Auden," in *Predilections*, 87.

14. Moore, "Anna Pavlova," in *Predilections*, 153.

15. Moore, "Feeling and Precision," in *Predilections*, 5.

16. Donald Hall, quoted on the jacket of Frank Bidart, *The Sacrifice* (New York: Random House, 1983).

17. Robert Hass, "Paschal Lamb," *New Poets of the Eighties*, ed. Jack Myers and Roger Weingarten (Green Harbor, Mass.: Wampeter Press, 1984), 124.

18. Theodore Roethke, quoted in Frank, *Louise Bogan*, 364.

19. Moore, "Compactness Compacted," in *Predilections*, 133.

20. Jonathan Miller, *The Body in Question* (New York: Vintage, 1978), 85.

21. Sukenick, "On Women in Fiction," 32.

22. Juhasz, *Naked and Fiery Forms*, 35, 350.

23. Moore, but I don't know which poem. I'm quoting from memory.

24. Roy Harvey Pearce, *The Continuity of American Poetry* (Princeton: Princeton University Press, 1961), 366.

25. Juhasz, *Naked and Fiery Forms*, 39.

26. Moore, "Idiosyncrasy and Technique," in *A Marianne Moore Reader* (New York: Viking, 1961), 170.

Adding to the Unhappiness
Those Poems You Are Writing

There are so few credible attacks on the state of contemporary American poetry that when one discovers a lonely voice on the horizon, one really hopes for an invigorating call to battle, or at the very least, that something gruesome and unknown about the situation might be crammed down our throats with the right authority.

I was hoping for this when I read the promising banner: "Poetry Cornered" with the subtitle, "Art for Art's Sake, but This is Ridiculous." The article was appearing in the *New Republic,* their writer in this instance—James Atlas.

The headline of the article proved, unfortunately, to be the kind of promise a boxer makes before entering the ring when he feels the crowd will simply appreciate that he's gotten into the ring with a mammoth and unbeaten opponent. There's a lot of dancing around and hanging off the ropes before final unconsciousness.

I was sorry to see Mr. Atlas devoting his undaunted attention to the paraphernalia of what he calls "the poetry hustle." This may be inflammatory news to those who read more about poetry than they read poetry, but for anyone seriously involved in the life that aspires to writing, reading, and supporting the kind of poetry one admires, it was odd to find so much energy spent lamenting the fact that one is able now to make a living from teaching the writing of poetry, thereby unleashing contagion upon the noble brow of Poetry.

Indeed, Mr. Atlas's first sentence is enough to strike terror into the heart of any stockbroker or dental assistant. "One thousand five hundred fifty poets are listed in the latest directory issued by Poets & Writers, Inc.," he says. This is about the size of my high school population. Imagine an entire high school of nothing but poets—poet cheerleaders, poet tuba players, poet pregnancies and dropouts. "Startling profusion," Mr. Atlas calls it, and already he is behind in the count with over two thousand poets listed six months later.

Mr. Atlas tells us that poetry has become merely "a lifestyle." Poets have become too resourceful. They've even solved their readership problem by inventing workshops, conferences, poetry buses, and readings. They are talking their poems shamelessly in classrooms and auditoriums. Poetry, once hard to come by and free, is now rampant and subsidized by government grants. In fact, this poetry conspiracy is dramatically pictured as "waves of poets," so one wants to rush out immediately and buy a dinghy.

Other targets of this article were the young art of poetry blurbs, the worldly- and otherworldly-ness of contributors' notes, and pictures of the poets in anthologies.

In spite of the peripheral nature of these concerns, I think Mr. Atlas was heading for an important punch, which he failed to deliver. There is, in fact, an immense amount of poetry being written which appears to have been written by the same person or by persons so like-minded as to call into question the very activity of writing and publishing poetry. Have we heard this before? Yes, often and tiresomely, but I would like to relate my own experience of this and try to bring the subject around to something more than a hysterical version of "The Russians Are Coming."

What amounted to a poetry whiteout for me occurred about a year ago when I read eighteen hundred manuscripts (ten pages each) from poets all over the country. I was one of the preliminary readers for the NEA Grants Committee and read all the submissions. Those I liked well enough to send on to the committee were then considered for the awards.

I talked to Joyce Carol Oates about having done this when we met at a conference where we were teaching in upstate New York. I said I hadn't been able to look at a poem or write one at the end of that four-month ordeal. We joked that I ought to sue the NEA for psychic damage.

But couldn't I tell right away which poems and manuscripts to read thoroughly? Weren't there some I could discount after a quick scan? Not really. Most of these writers possessed the facility for *seeming to engage* the reader with a high degree of skill and life savvy. This made it impossible to discount anything quickly. The surfaces of these structures looked like poems one should not take lightly. But once inside the poems, I found myself thinking of those decorated eggs whose insides have been sucked out to retard spoilage so that the surface might be painted with designs. Pictures of fashion models with glassy looks and classy clothes, an air of disinterested melancholy. These also give some idea of what I often felt reading these manuscripts.

In the end, I saved for myself only seven full manuscripts which I thought especially interesting (though I sent on considerably more to the committee) and a dozen or so single poems. What I admired of those I saved was that the feeling had not been finished out of them. Something mattered and I would be brought to feel it. Whether they were writing of lived and/or imagined experiences, these poets were moving toward and finding consequence. I don't mean to imply that something one experiences in the imagination alone is not "lived." It is, but with another credibility than that for which one has actually born the blows, psychically, physically and emotionally. As Ciarán Carson, a young Irish poet, recently wrote me from Belfast, "There is often too much attention given to the unlived life." At the end of a good poem one would like to feel as moved as the narrator of the great Frank O'Connor short story, "Guests of the Nation," when he says in the last line, "And anything that happened to me afterwards, I never felt the same about again."

Looking over these saved poems, I see that many would not be appreciated by a non-poetry-reading public. They appeal to my love of the difficult, are not quickly accessible, are, I suppose, "hermetic." Yet I would not forego these for those eager others. If the voice is interesting enough, I extend all kinds of credit, postpone my judgment. By the third and fourth readings, I may still be uncovering surprises in the poems that truly engage me. This is not against "art," but anyone without patience would think so.

There is a variety of poetry, quite different from that I have just mentioned, which I have called elsewhere "paper-plate poetry." It is disposable after one reading. The language, content, and music do not return the reader to the poem. The poets I enjoy most are usually attracting a return by giving me more than I can handle the first time around and not just through being oblique. I may have the feeling I've missed something while at the same time I may also have a clear reading on an initial level. There are poets who are very good at display, lots of fireworks and dislocations, but if it's just a kind of working off of energy, its excitement is partial, like that of dreams whose events are colorful but which represent parts of a beautiful machine whose use and contours are withheld.

Donald Hall in his fine book of reminiscences, *Remembering Poets,* speaks of Dylan Thomas as "the maddest of word-mad poets." But this was an important first step in the poet's development, a step toward the love of words which includes what Hall calls "pursuit of the spirit." Because this pursuit is at the heart of what one might ask of the poetry scene at large now, the following passage from *Remembering Poets* is worth quoting in full so that we might relocate for ourselves the relationship between the spirit and words. Hall says:

> All poets start from loving words, and loving to play with them. Then they learn to love poetry as well, or the Muse herself, and make poems from this love of poetry—hoping to add new stars to the heaven. But the great poets as they turn older look past the Muse—who is objectified taste, composed of all great poems of the past—to pursue vision, to discover motions of spirit and of human consciousness, which it is art's task to enlarge. Sometimes a poet developed past the love of words will lose poetry altogether, will disavow language in favor of vision—and write endless boring theological sonnets like Wordsworth's. Often the best poems happen when lines cross; the poet writes in pursuit of the spirit, while words still roar with years of obsession and love. The luckiest poet is like

Yeats; from the time he could say that he sought "an image, not a book," he kept words and vision together.

What kept me from dismay with the bulk of the manuscripts I read for the NEA was a patience with *becoming*. Most of these writers were my own age or a bit younger. They deserved, after all, the same hope one gives from poem to poem in one's own work, the hope that some interior light will cause the words to shine on the life. So very much of art is outside manipulation, belongs more to the instinct of the moment, luck and aspiration, this last being in much need of restoration these days.

I am always on the lookout for what may inspire a worthy attitude toward the writing of poetry. Usually I come upon signs quite by accident, just a willingness to follow out hunches. Lately I've been reading a little book by Albert Camus called *Lyrical and Critical Essays*. I'd like especially to mention one chapter, "On a Philosophy of Expression by Bruce Parain." Parain was a writer who was politically close to Camus late in Camus's career. Camus says of him, "Parain's basic idea is one of honesty: the criticism of language cannot get around the fact that our words commit us and that we should remain faithful to them. Naming an object inaccurately means adding to the unhappiness of this world. And, in fact, the vast wretchedness of man . . . is falsehood."

These errors in naming, one begins to understand, are those which cause us to see in ways that cut us off from faithfulness to the words as they are attached to the world and those in the world we must speak to, of, and with. Poets, because their medium is language, must engage the falsehoods as much as the truths, for language "is neither true nor false," says Camus. "It is simultaneously useful and dangerous, necessary and pointless. . . . Neither yes nor no, language is merely a machine for creating doubt." Reading this last, I had that "Oh, so-this-is-what-you've-been-doing" feeling. "Doubt" hovered. If disbelief and uncertainty are, indeed, the provinces of the poet, then it is no wonder they often seem only fleetingly intelligible to what Auden called "the odious public." Many readers of poetry are disappointed that the crisp logistics of a Donne, the wary folk wisdom of Frost, and the intelligent question-as-answer in Dickinson have been traded for the wavering of poets often trying to convince themselves they have anything at all to say. These new poets are depending heavily on the innate capacity of language to provide its own subject matter once it is set in motion. Camus says that Parain only "glimpses" the fact that language is always out there ahead of us and "contains a power that reaches far beyond ourselves." Poets, of course, always know this instinctively, unlike philosophers who seem forever trying to get ahead of the language.

Camus defines the battle lines in the struggle for meaning in a way that perhaps explains the recent shift from Stevens's "not ideas about the thing, but the thing itself" to something more like: "Ideas *are* the thing itself and *more* than the thing itself." In the work of John Ashbery and some other writers experience and "idea" have become simply a quality of mind so that "about" becomes a kind of location in itself. Camus says:

> Either, in fact, our words translate only our impressions and, partaking of their contingency, are deprived of any precise meaning; or else our words represent some ideal and essential truth, and consequently have no contact with tangible reality, which they can in no way affect. Thus we can name things only with uncertainty, and our words become certain only when they cease to refer to actual things.

So an aesthetic for accommodating the uncertainty of language develops out of a mistrust for words as they fail to approach our experience of the world.

This word *contingency* seems especially appropriate to the contemporary flavor of poetry. It indicates an extreme of that propensity of all poetry to *verge* on saying without saying. Only in the modern mode, land is often never in sight. The reader comes away with a sense of having traveled without arrival, except in purely aesthetic ways, a sensation for initiates to the art not unlike seasickness. Often poets seem to write as though what they say does not have the power to affect what Camus calls "tangible reality"; that is, the meaning of our lives and how we live them. And this is a true enough feeling that we have no power whatsoever over incredible structures prepared to destroy not only entire continents but the entire planet. Perhaps it represents a kind of unconscious or conscious despair which causes poets to settle into a kind of drone, words communing with words to the extent that their human context is ignored or only slightly present.

Camus reminds us of Socrates' much more fearful regard for the extent to which language affects one's being when he said in the *Phaedo:* "The misuse of language is not only distasteful in itself, but actually harmful to the soul." Just as the soul has fallen into as much disregard as our hope in language to provide a step toward reason, it has had a hard time making us accountable to our lives. We can't be properly afraid for its journey here, though certainly we should be. For the ultimate sign of our disbelief in our own souls is our inability to believe in the souls of anything else around us. Against this disbelief, James Wright mourned for the dying Ohio River, and Richard Hugo witnessed the deaths of whole towns in Montana. We read Marianne Moore's poems about animals on the verge of extinction not just because we're sentimental and want to go on like Noah's ark with two of everything, but because she reminds us of the exotic in such a way that we reach its sacredness, its difference to the world.

Talk of the soul seems strangely appropriate in the face of Mr. Atlas and his worry over "the poetry hustle" and whether or not there is any readership for the onrush of poetry being turned out by poetry workshops, prison inmates, children, the elderly, mental patients, Vietnam War veterans, therapy groups at large, and others of the disenfranchised. It's probably true that poetry has often been misused in an effort to help people's lives. If so, Mr. Atlas should be glad the readership of such poetry is often self-contained within the group of origin . . . or cast gaily upon the water in the myriad of little magazines.

I don't believe myself there is certain loss to the highest ambitions we may have for poetry just because it attracts those in need of therapy through approaching the self in poetic form. It might be too frightening to impose a care for one's soul upon such groups. Imagine the voice rising in the midst of a poetry workshop to ask of the young poet, "But do you realize, this sort of poem could be harmful to your soul?" No, probably the real work of poetry has to be done without speaking that word, though it underlies everything we want to give ourselves to in the name of worth.

Joyce Carol Oates writes more substantially and sympathetically than Mr. Atlas in a later article in the *New Republic,* the December 9, 1978, issue. She speaks also of the reputed lack of a readership for poetry. I say "reputed" because no one actually has a true account of how much poetry is being bought and read, though it seems the readers one meets are all writers. I remember some much-talked-about figures which showed that a leading poet's latest book had sold five hundred copies, or that of hundreds who submitted to a contest, few bought the prize-winning volume—bad sportsmanship to say the least. On the other hand, I also know of an instance of a first book handled by a small press having sold nearly four thousand copies and now heading toward a third edition. This would be an indication that there is strong readership of one sort or another out there for some writers just beginning their careers.

Ms. Oates reminds us that poetry has always been "difficult." And well it might be, since it is language and life in its most concentrated form. Ms. Oates says of the books under review in her article that she is "struck by a common element of technical accomplishment that is 'sophisticated'—in the best sense of that word—and also by an appeal, a raw and almost frightening appeal, that the reader share in the deepest, most private intimacies of the poet's soul." There we are again, back with that word soul, given by dictionaries to mean "the immaterial essence of an individual life." Immaterial is meant to signify spiritual, not the ironic secondary meaning of immaterial, which is "trifling" or "unimportant," though the overlap is relevant. Ms. Oates makes the distinction between prose and poetry that prose "dilutes emotion" while poetry speaks directly and frankly of emotion. She says, "All poetry is confessional. The poet's self speaks to the reader's self, and though they are often separated by history, geography, and gender, there is no mistaking the pang, the shock, of kinship." This sometimes invasive intensity keeps the readership of poetry small, says Ms. Oates. She observes that most people do not want to enter into the intensities of other lives and one wants to add, often not even their own. They read to be entertained. "One does not always *want* to be as moved as, say, the reader of Adrienne Rich's *Dream of a Common Language* will be." So there is the idea that you have to be emotionally athletic to be a poetry reader.

My own idea of the best poetry is that it doesn't speak directly of emotion, but it certainly *embodies* it in a higher concentration than most fiction, since everything usually happens within the space of a page or two. This sort of poetry is most compelling because it is not just waddling around the duck pond, billing up a little water now and again and pausing to quack reproachfully or mournfully at the onlookers. However, in a scene as diverse as the American one, one finds also a milder, more meditative sort of poetry. But the poems which seem to admit readers of all types and experience are still narrative in structure and often deal with family or other love relationships. When I give books of poetry, as I often do, to friends not regularly reading or writing poetry, these story poems are the ones they most often respond to.

Contrary to a "well-if-you-get-it, OK, if-not, OK" attitude among poets I came along with through the early seventies, poets in the last two years have begun to admit to me that they would like to be read by those other than their pals and those singularly involved with poetry. One said, "I'd like a secretary, for instance, to be able to pick up my book and be able to understand it." Secretaries are mistakenly thought to be congenial coolies who are good spellers and can answer a flurry of random needs while at the same time assessing minute fluctuations in the daily presences of those they must assist. What better training for the reading of poetry! My own experience with secretaries on the university scene has been that they are as sensitive and open as those they work for, and often more so. I saw asking for a less specialized audience for poetry as a rise in ambition rather than any lowering of sights, then.

When Randall Jarrell lamented, "God has taken away our readers and given us students," he was perhaps unfair to students. They are industrious readers and have the time in their lives to give a second and third reading to a poem. They are often as omnivorous as the offering allows, so many different kinds of poems can get a fair reading. And there are signs that they enjoy it these days, unlike the old force-feeding days. There is strong evidence that writing programs (and I have participated extensively in five with a hand in designing two of these, and have visited at least fifty other programs on reading tours) have been instrumental in saving many English programs because they return the writers to the reading of the literature of all periods. This is contrary to Mr. Atlas's feeling that many poets of the workshop variety, as most are these days, have not read *The Waste Land.* With so many trying desperately to write, it's certain that there are those who don't read enough. Writing programs which don't require or encourage a knowledge of literature, past and present, are certainly at fault, though this is such an assumed part of a writer's knowledge that perhaps this has caused its omission as a requirement at the graduate level at some schools. I know at Iowa, the writers often arrive in their mid-twenties after having earned master's or doctoral degrees in English elsewhere. The referential nature of the best writing classes should quickly humble anyone who doesn't know the literature.

Both Ms. Oates and Mr. Atlas point to the need for more stringent and responsible criticism of poetry. Ms. Oates characterizes what criticism we do have as "self-referential, self-serving and vaporous." Mr. Atlas, on the other hand, takes these qualities in the affirmative and says that poets should be at least as self-serving as their forefathers. He says, "In the past, poets often have taken it upon themselves to ratify their own work by means of literary criticism. How few contemporary poets, by comparison, have worked at critical prose, a chore that occupied virtually every English and American poet from Dryden to Coleridge, from Arnold to Pound, Lowell, Ransom, Tate and other poets of that generation. . . ." He characterizes the "statements on poetics" in Donald Allen's *The New American Poetry* as nothing more than "vatic pronouncements upon the nature of language."

If Mr. Atlas has read the criticism of Stevens, Marianne Moore, Bogan, Jarrell, and Eliot, he must be aware that this concern for the nature of language is at the center of what they often want to speak about. Take, for example, the titles of some of Moore's essays: "Feeling and Precision," "A Grammarian of Motives: A Poet in What He Says and in Knowing How What is Said Has Been Said," and "A Machinery of Satisfaction." But perhaps the scene could use someone more like Pope, whose poems were themselves political responses to what he found distasteful among his literary enemies.

It is rare to find vehemence on the scene, except perhaps the tiresome mention of the Iowa Mafia. Enemies? Not really, just preference. However, I suspect that if critics want to get scrappy, there will be enough writers with equal spunk to take them on. One must remember, when wondering why there aren't more poet-critics, that Eliot was not teaching poetry workshops. Those poets who might teach three to five poetry writing sessions a week use up their critical energy on those close at hand. When they have time to themselves, they prefer to read other poets and write their own poetry. They don't have the need to promote an argument for their view of what poetry should be in the scene at large. They usually have a following at hand and a forum for dressing down anything they don't care for on the spot.

In my Camus readings I found that he was writing essays for publication as early as age nineteen. He had a sense that he had a right to speak and had something valuable to say. This kind of confidence is hard to get on the contemporary poetry scene. Its diversity of approaches in a single same-sounding voice tends to level what thoughts one has about it. As an Irish poet visiting me recently said, "If I were writing over here it would take me a long time to know where I was." The elders don't say much because they are busy judging poetry contests, running writing programs or traveling to give readings and yes, writing poems. Poetry conferences seem to be the place where the real contentiousness comes out. Views are given and attacked. Personalities clash and lobby for sympathy among the initiates. In the best of these, there is still a modicum of good humor and professional respect maintained, whatever the views. But where in the magazines does one go to get good, well-written, and intelligent criticism of a broader scale?

I think Herb Liebowitz has high standards and publishes many fine writers in *Parnassus,* which is devoted entirely to essays and reviews of poetry. The *Quarterly Review of Literature,* edited by Theodore and Renee Weiss, is also very good. A voice I've been impressed with is Denis Donoghue's. He also publishes in the *New Republic.* In fact, the *New Republic* might be a magazine to keep an eye on. Its "Correspondence" section after Mr. Atlas's article appeared shows that a few people concerned with good criticism and the state of poetry already read the magazine. One of these, David Kirby, I think spoke well in reminding Mr. Atlas that while there are indeed the two groups he describes, "the vast number of talentless poets who publish and promote themselves because no one else will do it for them, and the several dozen name poets who live mainly in the northeast, who are published by New York and Boston firms," there is also another group, which Kirby estimates as a hundred or so, who are among the most interesting writers and who are publishing fine work in the literary magazines and in the small presses. Ms. Oates's article also honors this group and rightfully laments the fact that many of them will never be heard from because so much of what little criticism is written goes toward the work of writers already established.

There are several small magazines in which I find good criticism regularly. Each reader will begin to think of his or her own list; these are a few I think to mention: the *Antioch Review, Canto, Ploughshares,* the *Georgia Review,* the *Iowa Review, Dark Horse, Quarterly West, Ironwood, Prairie Schooner, Salmagundi,* the *Hudson Review,* the *Black Warrior Review,* and essays in the special issues of *Antaeus*—one in particular entitled "Poetry and Poetics" by Robert Haas, others by Stanley

Kunitz and Paul Fussell. Most poets I know seem more interested in poetics than they are in brow-beating whatever literary enemies they might fabricate or dredge up. They prefer not to expose themselves as belonging too firmly to this or that group, if indeed groups can really be located. They would rather write the next good poem than dignify opposing camps, if they did exist, with an attack. The young writers know that NEA awards and other contests are judged by other poets, so biting the wrong hand could mean no fellowship, no publication, no readings, no teaching job. This may partially explain the slack-hearted, overintricate maneuvers in which a writer examines a poet's work only on its own ground but does not take it farther into the arena of what is being done by others. If a poet does speak about the work of his or her fellow poets, it's probably going to be someone whose work is close to him; and friendship between them is not unlikely. And it would be a bad state of affairs indeed if one could not present the work of a friend one admired.

Perhaps we are waiting for those bright and brave new readers, those who aren't necessarily writers and who are beholden to no one, to put us soundly in our places. Criticism or giving one's opinion on any scale is a thankless task, but a much-needed one. We may be heading for a time when the glut of poetry will cause more would-be writers to put their talents to work in the less-crowded field of appraisal. Until then, there will be more poems to read silently in the chair by the window, some of them poems that speak in a way that returns the calm, like the poem I'd like to close with, "January Visit," by Laura Jensen. It was written on a visit Jensen made to Port Angeles, Washington, and talks about a walk we took along a beach near my home. I like the poem's simplicity, its confidence in using the landscape at hand, our place in it. I think the non-poetry-reading public could appreciate this poem, be enriched by the sign at its conclusion, though this ease is not, of course, what insures our interest. Rather, accessibility is a by-product of the events at hand having been presented clearly and at the same time mysteriously. The white circle on a stone causes an imaginative X-ray vision in the poet which carries the white mark of purity and trust, this stone's difference to those who hold it, clear through. Suddenly there is a reason for having picked up that particular stone.

January Visit

Friday morning on the beach
you stalked back up the tracks
to find your leather gloves.
I thought you had left me
by the train-sized FLAMMABLE drums
down the rails from the mill.
We had come a fair way between the sound
of rocks tumbling under waves
and the green weeds frozen
in clear pools, in silence
my bent stick could not shatter.
Everywhere, there was hoarfrost.

The last thing you would do
would be to give me something
I could write about. So I dropped
my magazine into the bus seat
and looked for my last sight of you
smiling, holding up your rock.
You had picked it up on the cold beach
Friday morning, dark gray
with a white ring, and I assume
the white passes through the rock
clean, unblemished, unblemishing
and signifies a good thing.

An Interview with
Rachel Berghash

In a number of poems you write about your father's death. Is writing these poems a way of grieving, a way of consoling, or a way of healing?

All of these things. I always think that poems are, maybe, the least expensive kind of therapy for many people. They've always been my secret church, the place I feel I can hear and reach other people and myself. A place where the meeting of those beautiful and hard times can take place. I have a colleague at Syracuse University, Hayden Carruth, who said to me after my father's death: "Pain plus time equals beauty." I think that poems are part of that alchemy—they're the beauty part, probably. I mean, even though it's very hard to tell these stories, the beauty is in the witnessing of the life, I think—the attempt to preserve the dignity of that life, even at the most painful and sad time of parting.

Your poems do attempt to transcend experience. I am wondering whether you're able to transcend such experience in your life too?

It takes a long while when someone so close to you dies. My father's death is still with me quite a lot. I remember on a trip

This interview was conducted in the offices of WBAI radio for the program "A World Elsewhere" in late spring of 1985. Rachel Berghash regularly produces this program, featuring contemporary poets and writers, for WBAI.

to China the summer after his death feeling: "Oh, why is he so close to me now; I'm in such a strange country; the strangest country I have ever been to." And yet I would look out at the landscape and feel very close to him during that whole time. You never know, of course, when that grief will revisit you. I think that writing the poems was very helpful to me in expressing my love for my father, as complicated as it is.

How do you identify with your father? You seem to be identifying with him especially in your poem "Black Silk."

He was a man who gave his entire life over to hard work. I feel that unless I had attempted to tell his story he might very much have disappeared. I remember the first time I felt that my poetry might be worth anything was when I wrote a poem called "Black Money" (it's in my first book), and my father recognized himself as the hero of the poem; and suddenly it was like, Well, you're doing something worthwhile after all. I think that this sense of children wanting to reach their parents is more all right than people admit. Sometimes people act like it's a shameful thing to be doing—to try to do something which pleases your parents. I managed to please my parents and please myself too. And it was very unexpected, because my father was a logger and later a longshoreman; and that he should ever respond to poems is an unusual thing. It gave me another kind of reach as a poet, to be trying to reach my father before he died, in the poems. It became my language for honoring and speaking to him. Because we had a very difficult time. He was alcoholic and had a lot of life frustrations that made living with him quite difficult.

Would you say then that you write poetry for your father? Very often we do things for *someone, in the sense that we keep the person in mind while doing a particular thing.*

Some of the poems. Yes. Especially in *Willingly,* my last book. I couldn't have told him that of course. I think now of the things I wanted to say when I knew he was going—I wish I had said to him: "I am going to write some wonderful poems for you." But you never know whether you will be given these poems. I do have the sense of being given the right to write certain poems. Some members of my family don't agree that I should have written a poem like "Accomplishment," which is about the actual moments of my father's dying. At least, I think, my mother felt this was a very private moment and shouldn't have been exposed. But the actual moment of the dying is so seldom written about, that I felt I had to do a kind of spiritual anatomy there; so I did write about it. I felt it was my right to. One of the things as a writer you can't always do is answer the wishes of other people.

In your poem "Woodcutting" you mention the lost mountains of your childhood. I was wondering what is most lost? And what in your past pleases you most?

I had a very idyllic kind of place in which to grow up, having been born and raised in the Northwest on the Olympic Peninsula. Since my father was a logger, I grew up in the logging camps and the clearings. It was very beautiful. You had trees around you and wild animals. I was never really involved in the hunting, but the stories, the storytelling around that was something I loved from my childhood. At first the family lived rather meagerly, but later I had a horse and some of the things that children want to have. I had a very free, and yet very responsible, childhood. Even our play was always somehow connected with work. I'd go out and collect pine cones, and we'd sell these for ten dollars a bag. Or we would collect beer bottles to sell. I'm talking about the kind of play we had to do to get money to put food on the table. There were five children in the family. Growing up among five children was a very rich experience. I'm just now getting to know my brothers and my sister again, because I've moved back to the Northwest where I'll be spending nine months of the year now. So my poems are starting to reflect this homecoming more, the beauty of this area. Coming from a beautiful place you kind of have to earn it back. I'm in the process of doing that, of saying: "Okay, I've seen the world and now I deserve where I was born." I'm able now to write more about my growing up; about going fishing with my father; about my mother who was my father's logging partner. I've just written a poem about her called "Present," which is her story of going out to log with my father and realizing on the mountain that she was carrying a child. I became that child. I'm proud of my background in the Northwest. I think it nourishes me. That's why I've returned. I like to live near the strait of Juan de Fuca and look out the window and see the eagle fly over every day. Also, I just enjoy looking out at the water. The closeness to water and that kind of moss-light in the Northwest is very important to me. It's a very subdued, rather Japanese-like light. It makes you very meditative and inward in a productive way. I don't know if I answered your question, but I told you some things about the Northwest.

It sounds very beautiful. As we get older, life becomes more complicated; the way you describe your life now, you've been able to simplify it so you can do what you want to do.

One thing that's made me most happy of late has been being able to make a life in the Northwest with the writer Raymond Carver. He was born in eastern Washington, which is very dry and flat compared to here. My brothers have taught him how to salt water fish for salmon, and he's come to love this place that I've loved all my life. He's written two books of poems from this area now, one called *Where Water Comes Together with Other Water* and a second entitled *Ultramarine*. He was mainly known as a fiction writer when we met. But he had written several books of poems, and since he's been with me, he's been writing more and more poems.

So you and the landscape evoke the poetic part of him.

Well, he really loves poetry, and I think being with a poet has probably encouraged him to devote himself to his poetry for longer periods of time.

*I am struck by your poem "Linoleum," by your "longing for religion."
You are on target when you write about the "loneliness of the
saints"—the loneliness of those who aim for perfection. Could you
comment on this?*

I've never really been able to be very orthodox. I feel re-
ligious, but I don't have a form for it except in my poems—a
rather nonsecular form of religion. I don't know what I
would have done if I hadn't had poetry; how I would have
expressed this part of myself. I suppose that there are many
artists who are like this. I've always mistrusted the superior
position that orthodox religion affords—that you have these
rules and you follow them and you'll be okay. My poem gives
a rather two-sided view of the Jains, an Eastern Indian re-
ligious sect that believes in being very careful and respectful
toward insects and all other living creatures, really. They use
brooms to sweep the ground so that they don't walk on any
insect, and they often cover their mouths so they don't acci-
dentally breathe insects in. And when they drink, they're
very careful about that too so as not to swallow insects. They
live at an extreme of concern that none of us could really
manage without entirely giving up the lives we live. But I
admire their attitude toward life and the things that they
strive for. I think, how wonderful also to have it really *down*
what one should strive for! Well, the Jains strive for these
very good things—and then you learn some contradictory
facts about them: that they're really in the business of lend-
ing money, and that they've made themselves very wealthy.
I like to have these contradictions in view—not for one to
cancel out the other, but so that the whole picture is before
me.

Linoleum

for Mark Strand

There are the few we hear of
like Christ, who, with divine grace,
made goodness look easy, had
a following to draw near, gave up
the right things and saw to it

that sinners got listened to.
Sharpening my failures, I remember
the Jains, the gentle swoosh
of their brooms on a dirt path
trodden by children and goats, each
thoughtful step taken in peril of
an ant's life or a fat grub hidden
under a stick. In the car-wash,
thinking of yogis under a tree
plucking hair by hair the head
of an initiate, I feel at least
elsewhere those able for holiness—
its signs and rigors—are at work.
Ignominiously, I am here, brushes
clamped, soap and water pulsing
against my car. (A good sign too,
those asylums for old and diseased
animals.) My car is clean
and no one has had to
lift a finger. The dead
bugs have been gushed away into a soup
of grit and foam—the evidence
not subterranean, but streaming along
the asphalt in sunlight so dazzling
I attend the birth-moment of
the word *Hosannah!*

I care about the bugs and not
in this life will I do enough towards
my own worth in the memory
of them. I appreciate the Jains,
their atonements for my neglect,
though I understand it makes poor farmers
of them, and good we all
don't aspire to such purity so
there's somebody heartless enough to
plow the spuds.

Early on in admiration, I put off
knowledge, and so delayed reading about
the Jains—not to lose
solace. But in the County Library,
turning a page, I meet them as
the wealthiest moneylenders

in Western India. Reading on,
I'm encouraged—the list of virtues
exceeds vices—just four
of those: anger, pride, illusion and
greed. The emphasis clearly on
striving. I write them down
in the corner of a map
of Idaho: forbearance, indulgence,
straightforwardness, purity,
veracity, restraint, freedom from
attachment to anything, poverty
and chastity.

Choosing, getting into the car to
get to the supermarket, hearing
over engine noise the bright agonies
of birds, the radio news with the child
nailed into a broom-closet for
twenty-four hours by parents who
in straightforwardness sacrificed
forbearance, I feel a longing
for religion, for doctrine swift
as a broom to keep the path
clear. Later, alone in the kitchen
with the groceries, I read the list
again. Overwhelmed by the loneliness
of the saints, I take up my broom
and begin where I stand,
with linoleum.

Also, you mention that one virtue is often sought at the expense of another.

Right. In "real life" you sometimes end up sacrificing one thing for another, no matter what your ideals are. "Values in Use" is a poem I love by Marianne Moore in which she reminds us that values are only as good as the use you put them to. So I'm always testing the value against what the outcome may be. Possibly that's my religion.

The word religion *comes from the Latin word* religio, *which means "to be tied to." Religion is something one is tied to, and you are tied to your poetry.*

Yes, that's a wonderful definition. I feel that every poem is a working out *not* of a doctrine, but of a root which is becoming obsolete even as I work it out. It's a path into an unexplored sector. I don't know if I will ever use it again. I follow it out in the time that it takes me to write the poem.

And you discover it while you are writing the poem, or do you spend time discovering it before writing?

I only discover it while writing. I think if I knew beforehand, I wouldn't be interested in writing. And sometimes I will finish a poem and I won't think it's right, I won't think I've gone far enough and so I rework that poem until I find that I've gotten some place that I didn't know I could reach. That's one of the things I often do when revising my poems. You're trying to think, "Well, did I go anywhere new as I came down to the finish?" I think the way in which you finish a poem is the most important place in the poem, the place where you're going to satisfy or disappoint the urges that got you to write the poem in the first place.

So you *have to be satisfied?*

Yes. *I* have to be satisfied. It doesn't matter if I satisfy an audience if I haven't satisfied myself. I won't ever be satisfied with that poem. I think there are some disingenuous moments in the poem "Linoleum," because I'm speaking kind of tongue in cheek. Even when I say "I have a longing for religion," I don't think I am entirely telling the truth. I do have a longing in the sense that I often wish I could settle important moral questions once and for all, but I don't have a longing for religion in the sense that I could ever adopt its methods entirely. It seems too static, finally.

Could it be that you don't have a longing for institutionalized *religion?*

Yes. That's it, of course.

But you do have a longing for some of the things that religion talks about, like virtues?

Yes, exactly. It's like the Idaho potatoes in the poem "Linoleum"—you have to dig to get them. You have to get your hands dirty, kill a few bugs, even accidentally. . . .

In your poem "In That Time When It Was Not the Fashion," you are "standing in the beloved past moments, so that nothing might be lost." Yet the poem ends without hope. Why?

In That Time When It Was Not the Fashion

When the daughters came for me
with their hands webbed in each other's hair,
when they saw, even to the last, how desire
kept me ripe, they grew tender
as the portraits of swans
whose necks are threaded on the open
pond. Their arms at my waist
were strong, were yearning.

We walked near the water's edge.
I told them the one story I called
my life as it began
when I looked back in that far place.

On the table in the land of hunters,
I said, there was meat
and it was eaten. I was born there
with brothers. They learned the ways
of the fathers, could take animals
unawares. Some with their bows
left many days and came to the fire
miraculous, the white deer
on their arrows carrying them far
into pardon. Others returned the same day
and leaned their guns
in the doorway. They were not deceived
about death. The elk hung
their golden heads in the dirt
of the shed. A long suddenness had
closed their eyes open. I
was a child with other children. We
crept up. Our house
had been blessed. We touched
the cold fur, the bald eyes.

My teeth were sharp. I could see the shape
of a leaf in the dark. In one bed
we slept and in the night
we held each other without words or
desire, my brothers now with wives.
Nearest blood that they were, my
changes drove them from me.
My hair was a veil at my back to catch
what looks would follow.

A tall man came into my life. He
liked to dance and be sung to. "Bend
to me," I said, "but not
too far. I like
to reach up." In a time
when it was not the fashion, I neglected
every good chance to live for myself
alone. "What
do you need?" I said. "What pleases
you?"

Even to those unfaithful, at some ripe
moment, I could refuse them
nothing. I sent letters
absolving what hurt they might fear
to have done me. I pledged, I
said, "You are remembered well."
When they brought their new, their old
loves to meet me, I embraced them, I
let my picture be taken in their company.
I learned, in short, to stand with them
in the beloved past moments
so that nothing might be lost.

I would give you hope
against all this if I could.
But I cannot. I have drunk insects
at night from the river. Nor
did I wait for the fruit to fall.
I walked without thinking who lives
in the ground, too many steps. Not even
my death will have me. I am old
and unfinished. Keep watch for me.
I will have children to give away.

That's a character speaking in that poem. Sometimes you just have to write down what you're told. "I would give you hope / against all this if I could. / But I cannot." And then the poem ends, "Keep watch for me. / I will have children to give away." I think that's rather hopeful. If you have enough children you can give them away. I think when she says: "I would give you hope / against all this if I could"—she's talking about all of the wrong turns she's had to take. That is, one *has* to take these "wrong" turns in one's life. This poem is again referring to my reading of the Jains at the point where the speaker, a woman, says, "I have drunk insects at night from the river." In other words, she couldn't avoid committing the sins against the earth on which she lived. She didn't wait for the fruit to fall, she picked it. She wanted those things and she took them, whether they were ready or not. And she walked "without thinking who lives in the ground." But if "even your death won't have you"—it's a pretty hard situation, right? Yet since she's "old and unfinished," she still seems to have things to do and that's a vigorous sign.

There is one thing regarding your question about hope which people are often mistaken about when it comes to poetry, and that is that they think a poem should settle everything, and that by the end of the poem, you should be on firm ground. I think quite often my poems don't leave you on firm ground. The speaker of "In That Time When It Was Not the Fashion" says "keep watch for me" as if she's coming again. Having "children to give away" means to have a future. I think that's what children are all about. And it's almost a threat when she says that—to end the poem on that idea: "I will have children to give away"—meaning I will have affected the world so profoundly that I will have many carriers of my future. Something like that. You can read this in several different ways. Maybe the speaker won't be able to care for these children and so will *have* to give them away. If you think of Brazil you know what it means not to be able to care for children. I was there just last summer and saw many children living in the streets. And when you think of it, that's a very hard vision. But it's true. It's happening. Poems aren't obliged to be optimistic. If that's all people are looking for I suppose they could just take a Valium. The things you have to see in a life *are* often hard. You have to give what you can see and hear in that particular voice that's coming to you when you write the poem.

Do you write poems in which you are moved by qualities exemplified in your background or did you learn to apply or appreciate them on your own?

My mother gave me just one rule—she didn't go to church, but she read the Bible, and that was the only book in the house—and that rule was: "Do unto others as you would have them do unto you." That's the one I try to work with, to empathize with other people to the degree that I can understand what would be wrong to do in a situation. For instance, to think, "I wouldn't want that to be done to me." Even so, you spend a lot of time failing to meet even such a seemingly simple commandment. I was raised with a lot of those good home staples of the Ten Commandments, but that's the main one. I have a friend, a Swiss scholar named Harold Schweizer, and he's fascinated with the fact that morality and moral values seem of little importance in contemporary American poetry. He's become interested in discovering which contemporary poets are interested in moral values, so he's writing a series of essays to explore this. I've just read his piece on Irving Feldman and find it quite wonderful.

Whenever I read your poems, I do feel more hopeful about life.

I think poems *can* give courage and hope. But there's no mandate for poems to simplify experience in order to do that. Sometimes the poem will simply be a portrait of unsolved fears.

In some of your poems you seem to be working out the terms of forgiveness. Is there a price to forgiving? Do you feel that there is a costliness to one's character?

You mean "I forgive you so kick me again, honey"? I see a lot of that. The person is so forgiving that they just don't care what happens to them. That's not a kind of forgiveness I am interested in.

No. I don't think anybody is, if they're sane enough. No, I'm thinking of a different kind of price—like loneliness. For instance, you may feel lonely when you are scrupulous about not wanting to hurt people, or when giving absolution.

I think loneliness is part of everybody's experience. Certainly, many of the young writers who come to study with me are writing poetry out of that very young loneliness—not the loneliness of having people leave them or of forgiving people, but say, the loneliness of having had to say "That's enough." Along with the forgiveness, you have to make decisions. In order to protect your own ability to forgive, you also have to realize what keeps that ability to forgive strong in yourself. Not to overtax it. Not to be foolish with it. I think it's a natural resource.

So you're saying there's a healthy and sane way of forgiving.

Yes. This is a country that pays a lot of attention to its physical well-being but doesn't do very much for its spiritual well-being. It doesn't do spiritual calisthenics. It's a country in which the adman can convince a whole country that everybody ought to be out jogging their five miles. In this country, you don't hear much about the things that could be nourishing us spiritually, except in those very tractlike, doctrinaire ways—the revivalists, for instance, who've found *"the* way" and want to inflict it on everybody else.

I couldn't agree with you more. Would you like to talk more about the lack of spiritual values in our culture?

I've called it "Soulocaust." That's my word for it. This country might be suffering from Soulocaust. Doris Lessing was in Australia at the time that Raymond Carver was there recently, and he brought a clipping of a news article in which she had been interviewed. She said that she was very tired of these

people in the audience after her readings asking her to be-
have like an oracle and give them answers to questions, both
in their personal lives and also in regard to world situations.
She said she was frustrated because the ways in which they
were asking these questions weren't ways which were going to
stimulate their own thinking. They wanted answers from *her*.
And I think this is a sign of the desperation of the times; that
people are looking for easy answers and wanting to be told,
rather than finding their own ways to solve the problems in
their lives, spiritually and actually. This is a time to be wary.
Because it's a time when someone irresponsible could come
before you and do just that—tell you what to do. And those
may not be the right things at all.

They could be very misleading.

I think that's why I trust the truth of poems more, because
they *don't* tell you. . . . They're not the hamburger-stands of
the soul. They are very complicated mechanisms, and what
they do is lead you into meditation, into finding your own
way. I don't want poetry that reminds me of fortune cookies.
Or, on the other hand, poetry that works as haphazardly as
opening the *I-Ching*. I don't like to be *that* lost.

*In your poem "Woodcutting on Lost Mountain" you say, "Maybe the
least loved / carries injury farther into tenderness / having first
passed through forgiveness." I think that's a complicated insight.*

That was written about my brother Morris who was perhaps
"the least loved" in our family. He was the oldest son. For
some reason or other, our father was awfully hard on him,
and ironically, he's the one I think who loved my father the
most, even more than I did, and who was the least able to
show it—he hadn't tried to articulate his love while my father
was alive. He became a logger, so that he's been emblem-
atically and actually reliving my father's life. He became a
"faller," which is the man who goes out and fells the trees. So
I think he did have to go farther than say, I did. Recently he's
written some beautiful poems for my father. I wish my father

had lived to read them. Ray [Raymond Carver] has dedicated his book, *Where Water Comes Together with Other Water,* to my brother and me. He appreciates my brother's ability to have gone through all this, and they've become friends.

You wrote a number of poems about horses. What do horses represent to you?

My grandfather raised horses, so I was around horses at a very young age. As a child, as a young girl, I even imagined I *was* a horse for some time. I used to go around neighing, and the horses used to answer me. When I went to China I had already been writing the poems about horses that were published in my book *Willingly.* That's why the horse appeared on the cover. But in China, I heard about a painter, who was a peasant and who'd gotten into the university by painting horses. All his life, he paid tribute to the horse, to thank the horse for giving him the privilege to study his painting. So somehow, I think I'll be writing poems all my life about horses—thanking them for the sense of beauty and vitality of spirit they allowed me to feel so early in my life.

Last Class with Roethke

There are those who, having known Roethke as friend, as fellow-teacher, or from several terms in the classroom, far outdistance me and my brief encounter with him. I was a member of the last class in poetry writing he taught at the University of Washington before his death in 1963.

I was eighteen years old and living away from home for the first time with a schoolmate from my high school. I was working two jobs and living mostly on apples and elk meat I had brought from home. I mention this as prelude to what I can say of Theodore Roethke as teacher because it may account for two probably un-American words which kept occurring to me in my thought of that time and since: the words *awe* and *privilege*. The first of these, *awe,* is the word which best describes the aura of Roethke's presence at the University of Washington. It preceded my entrance into his class. I felt it in the hallway near that classroom which overlooked the greenhouse. When Roethke blustered into the room, it was there. When I got up to leave the room, there was a weakness in the knees, a high racy queasiness in the chest. This ability to be affected physically by an activity and a presence has seldom happened since. I say "seldom" not to say "never" and wholly discredit myself with the truth.

I had cautioned myself prior to writing down anything about this experience. This was one of the things I wanted to avoid doing—falling into a worshipful attitude. I would definitely not speak about "awe." What could it have to do with teaching? It certainly was not something one could predict or make use of as a method to pass on to other teachers and if anything, it would only make of this a special instance to be approached with reverence—or worse, nostalgia. Nonetheless, I have put this notion of awe before myself and others perhaps because it has been so noticeably absent in my experience of teachers in and out of the classroom since that time with Roethke. But I must add that it was not awe for Roethke alone but for Roethke in his attitude toward the teaching of poetry, Roethke in his seriousness about poetry—this was what physically and psychically affected his students, I believe. I say psychically because I would not be writing today perhaps if this seriousness had not carried the power to haunt. Just to reassure you, this is not proceeding to a testimonial on the prospect of tapping a new resource we could call ghost power. However, it is important to say that I was ghosted by this encounter. That is, I was unequal to most of what was offered at the time it was given. What I experienced as a result of the class was a kind of retroactive preparation for an event which was already past.

I did not really begin to write poetry until 1969 . . . some six years later. During that time I lived in a state of dormancy. It was a time during which I made few attempts to actually write poems, but my thoughts were continually directed toward that aim. I was reading everyone Roethke had mentioned: Bogan, Yeats, Hughes, Lowell, Hall, Dickey, Donne, Dryden, Pope, Tennyson, and a host of others. Mentioning them in a list reminds me that he gave one the sense of all these writers coexisting. I did not feel that Pope was "back there" in time, but that he was presently relevant. The term "contemporary" did not lead the way in what was valued as it so overwhelmingly does in creative writing classes today. There was only one book required for the course, and it has remained an enigma to me ever since: It was *The English Galaxy of Shorter Poems* from Everyman's Library. Why this book? I have asked myself. It begins with Anon and finishes with Houseman. Roethke seldom referred to it, though once in my own case he took a prescription from it. "Your rhythms are too irregular, dear. I want you to memorize 'Tears Idle Tears' by next week." By the next week he would have forgotten, but I would have memorized the poem.

Each Friday Roethke required us to write out a poem we

had memorized. Usually we chose the poem, but sometimes he would dictate the memorization to a specific need. One of us would be asked to recite our poem aloud. I remember my chagrin the time he called on me and I had unluckily learned Hecht's "The Dover Bitch." All the time I was saying it aloud, I feared the eventual pronouncement he would make when it was over. "Not bad, dearie. We'll get you a spot on Broadway." Or on another occasion, when I had memorized all of "The Idea of Order at Key West" and another student who was his sometime tennis partner had also memorized something from Stevens, we were dubbed "you Stevens fans" and made to feel as though we had blundered out of the fold.

To return to that other un-American word, *privilege,* seems appropriate after acknowledging Roethke's grudging response when he glimpsed that any of us might prefer the poems of another contemporary poet to his own. He regarded us jealously at times—as he said in the notebooks—as one might regard a wife. We were to keep him first in our affections and although we were responsible in the nature of the craft to acquaint ourselves with these other writers, they were to be seen as supporting characters to Roethke himself.

This undemocratic sense of being privileged to be a member of the class came about partly because the class was limited to twelve members who were to be chosen by Roethke. I had unwittingly attempted to enter the class in spring term. The class had already proceeded through fall and winter, tackling first the three-beat, then the four-beat line. Spring term would be spent on iambic pentameter. Most of the members were continuing. In that first session of spring term there were perhaps twenty or more hopeful students cowering around the long seminar table and lined against the walls when Roethke entered. He plunged immediately into scare tactics I now recognize as calculated to run out all those who hadn't at least the stamina to withstand the force of his personality and the intensity he wanted to bring to the study of poetry. He went all the way around the table asking us each to give our cumulative grade point averages, saying "Not enough, honey," when it fell below 3.0. He made the task seem impossibly difficult. And for my benefit: "You'll have to be a goddamn genius to make it through the term if you haven't been here fall or winter term." We submitted our poems and shuffled out hopelessly. When the list of the twelve names was posted at the doorway of the classroom I could not even get near enough to read my name, but it was shouted back over the heads by a friend who hadn't made it. If the list had designated those who would form an expedition into the Antarctic, I think I would not have felt more unequal to the task as I imagined it. I felt some mistake had been made in my favor, that although I was unworthy of the company, some allowance had mysteriously been made. It was the first time I had ever been *chosen* to do anything I considered of consequence. I went immediately to Roethke and told him I was not ready. I would study and read over the summer and come again in the fall. He looked at me balefully in the way I have seen cows look at their calves and said, "If you're coming, dear, come now."

In the opening class, one of those students who had been excluded was to appear as a specter to the twelve assembled there. This student had made the mistake of plagiarizing from poems she thought had been forgotten . . . Genevieve Taggart's "The Enamel Girl" was one of the poems. Anyhow, Roethke was cut to the quick by this, not because the student had plagiarized, but because she had insulted him by thinking he would not recognize the poems in their altered state. "She's even improved on these guys," he said, reading first a poem by the dead poet and then the new version by the student. "She'll never get into a class of mine again," he said, and it was as though the gates of heaven had shut suddenly with an awful clang, forever. Why she thought she had to do this seemed beyond his comprehension. How could she imagine that he would not catch her? Did she think so little of him as a poet, as a teacher? We quivered in her shame and waited for his indignation to subside.

Along with this sense of privilege came a gradual divestment of our individual personalities. Although these were well honored in our poems, we found even our names disappearing in the group. Roethke invented pet names by which he domesticated us with some emblematic endearment. Two older women were called "mother" and various of the other women were "kitten," "petunia" or "pussycat" interchangeably. I don't remember that he applied such names to the male members of the class. The effect on me was that I felt at once intimate and appropriated, unknown, private, yet involved in the class as a consciousness apart from any other activity I had known. I felt, perhaps mistakenly, that Roethke had a personal interest, a stake in my future as a poet. As another poet and I talked of this recently, he pointed out that this was a terribly unfair and hard bargain to strike with students, most of whom were not equipped to deliver poems of sufficient quality to justify a career as a poet, so that some of Roethke's students may have been haunted far beyond their capabilities and even desires. If there are those whose lives Roethke ruined with aspiration, I can well imagine it, though it has to be one of the lesser crimes of an era.

My own reaction when the class ended that spring was one of self-dissatisfaction. I had written nothing I could admire. I think that in writing classes today the effect is generally quite the opposite—the students do manage to write one or two poems with which they can be pleased. But because of my experience with Roethke, in which the main value was in some earnestness of intent and effort toward the writing of poems, I began to doubt the easy gratification, in which the young writer writes something resembling a poem and goes forth thinking, "I am a poet." As teachers of poetry know, we are all too able to get poemlike structures from our students. What Roethke seemed to be aiming at intuitively was the more pervasive development of a sense of music and rhythm and also a deep commitment to the study and writing of poetry. The idea was that there might be some good lines and images but maybe no whole poems for a long while. I came, by some unspoken mandate, to want to write nothing short of my best. And this was the genius of Roethke's teaching for me.

I've since felt that Roethke was an intuitive teacher, a term which covers the impression that he seemed often unprepared, or struggling to articulate in such a way that I was surprised to find him brooding about his classes in the notebooks. His last classes seemed composed on the spot, haphazard even. He often seemed distracted or to have great difficulty in being with us, or at least I felt apologetic and burdensome and wished *for* him that he could be elsewhere. I have met many poets since who are teachers of poetry with surer, flashier techniques and methods, even some with lesson plans for the spirit, but the sort of impersonal yet intimate accompanying presence Roethke was and is, has not again occurred.

To Work and Keep Kind
A Tribute to Stanley Kunitz

Of the multitude of spoken and unspoken injunctions handed on from parents, teachers, and friends, there are a simple few the heart selects and pursues with an instinctive recognition. My title comes from Stanley Kunitz's plea to the ghost of his father at the end of the poem "Father and Son":

> O teach me how to work and keep me kind.

It is just these necessities I've seen Stanley Kunitz exemplifying to young writers over the past twelve years.

The character of Kunitz's own work and his dedication to the work of writers whose talents he has encouraged over the years, continues to inspire and amaze me. The impression is of an energy not unlike that of the salmon he writes so movingly about in "King of the River":

> dare to be changed
> as you are changing now
> into the shape you dread
> beyond the merely human.

His energy is indeed full of changes, of transformations informed by that final knowledge of our human fatedness which commands us, as he says in the poem, to "increase and die." His faith in my own endeavors to write poetry and to teach has been a guiding force at the very heart of my writing and living.

The first time I heard Kunitz's name was when Theodore Roethke read aloud to us a Kunitz poem entitled "The Science of the Night" in the spring of 1963. After Roethke's sudden death that summer Stanley Kunitz came to the University of Washington to read his poems in a special program to commemorate Theodore Roethke. It was the fall of 1963. I had just been swept away as only the young can be by the vision of a life dedicated to the writing of poetry. All summer I'd been washing dishes at night in a restaurant. Days I worked in the newsroom of my hometown paper as a reporter and girl Friday, hoping to be able to afford to return to college. On the occasion of Mr. Kunitz's reading, I was dispirited. Sick at heart. Roethke was gone.

When Kunitz was ushered into the packed lecture hall and seated in the chair directly in front of mine, it was as if an emissary from Roethke had suddenly arrived. I was so shaken by the sense of this that I remember thinking I should ask Mr. Kunitz to sign his book of poems for me—a daring act indeed since I had denied myself such a request of Roethke out of an assumption that this was probably beneath his dignity. But I was too far gone in need to honor such a scruple now. Nonetheless, my hand refused to make the short reach over the back of the chair to proffer the book. I'm laughable to myself in that moment, but caught too by the earnestness of such attachments to those who shepherd anyone's first tottering gestures in the attempt to write. Not until thirteen years had passed would my hand extend the same book of poems into those of Mr. Kunitz.

But the voice that gave his poems that day, full of unsentimental consequence and self-mended yearning, seems to have imprinted itself onto my psyche. I know now, as I didn't then, that the deep recognitions I felt had to do most probably with our common search for our fathers. Kunitz's own father had died as a suicide in a public park the spring before he was born. My father was alive, but distanced from me by drinking and spiritual torments which divided him from everyone. While Kunitz attempted to resurrect his father in order to gain the time they'd never had, I seemed pitted against the clock of my father's life in an effort to construct a language of the heart that would, I hoped, reach him and consequently my own life, before it was too late.

By comparison, I had a bounty of time with my father; and because I seized on my task early, I think my poems finally did give solace to my father. Yet since his death, I've felt closer to the mysterious ramifications of the loss Kunitz must have lived from the start. There is the cold withdrawal at the end of "Father and Son" as the father's ghost turns toward his son "the white ignorant hollow of his face." And, in a similarly eerie moment, the ghost of Abraham Lincoln coexists with a contemporary likeness which bears his "rawboned, warty look, / a gangling fellow in jeans" and then gives way to "that other one / who's tall and lonely." Kunitz has been haunted a lifetime by the sense of one who has been banished forever from the kingdom of the living. Perhaps this is what gives his poems such a strong reserve of mystery—this feeling of presences which have the power to outlast their corporeal forms.

Recently I used the word *mystery* in speaking to a group of writing students in Urbana, Illinois, and they looked at me as if I'd just suggested they all dig wells and drink only well water from that day forward. Mystery in poems seemed an anachronism. "I need my grottoes," I said. There was a blank look on their faces. At this point I reached for Kunitz's book of essays, *A Kind of Order, A Kind of Folly,* turned to the chapter entitled "Seedcorn and Windfall," and read to them:

> Poets today tend to be clearer—sometimes all too clear. A poem is charged with a secret life. Some of its information ought to circulate continuously within its perimeter as verbal energy. That, indeed is the function of form: to contain the energy of a poem, to prevent it from leaking out.

It is this sense of a secret inner life which nourishes the poems, signals its taboos and rituals as they limit or instruct access, that I value in Kunitz's poetry and person. Yet this containment never intends to obfuscate meaning arbitrarily. His mysteries arrive without exertion as a natural extension of his spirit-finding voice.

In 1973 I was attending classes at the Iowa Writers' Workshop when I purchased Kunitz's translations of Anna Akhmatova. I had so far not found a female poet in English who wholly captured my imagination. Akhmatova, through

Kunitz, came powerfully alive for me. I sat at the kitchen table in the small upstairs apartment and began the poem "Stepping Outside." It was directed to Akhmatova, telling her how she had allowed me to face some of the hardships of my life through her own example of strength. In a rush of gratitude I typed the poem and sent it off to Stanley Kunitz, whom I had never met.

Having since received many such gifts myself from those who've read my poems or essays, I now understand what a rare thing it was when I took from my mailbox a reply from Kunitz. So often the best intentions to thank or to inquire further toward such volunteer correspondents have been delayed or have escaped me altogether in the rush of travel or teaching. All the more to wonder at the magnanimous reply he made, asking me to send more poems for publication in the *American Poetry Review*. It was to be my poetic debut—the first time a group of my poems would appear in a poetry magazine with a large national circulation. I felt "discovered," and the loneliness of my strivings seemed, at last, to have won an advocate.

Three years later I was able to arrange a meeting when Kunitz accepted an invitation to read his poems at Kirkland College in upstate New York. I had just joined the teaching staff there. My personal life was a shambles. I was recently divorced from my poet husband and was unsure what I should do next. Kunitz arrived sans luggage, sans poems. I remember our first task together was to search in the library for periodicals which carried his most recent poems. We talked all the while of Roethke, and I remember a feeling of childlike jubilation on my part—not that of meeting, but of reunion. This visit, crucial as it was, renewed my resolve toward my own writing and confirmed me in the steps I had just taken to leave my unhappy marriage. The fresh reserve of energy that allowed me to leave America for Ireland shortly afterward also had something to do with the encouragement Kunitz had given me. There I was to write most of the poems which formed the heart of my second book, *Under Stars*.

Since then an intimacy so akin to that of father and daughter has developed that I fear mentioning it as such.

Maybe I'm afraid it is some spell which allows this inheritance. Also, I know I'm not the only beneficiary. I have good sisters in his affection—Louise Glück, Carolyn Forché, Cleopatra Mathis, Mary Oliver, Olga Broumas—my friends and some of the leading poets of my generation. And there are others— Michael Ryan, Daniel Halpern, Robert Hass, Gregory Orr— writers who have likewise benefited from his wisdom and support.

I remember his journey to the Northwest in 1978 for a writers' conference in Port Townsend, and how he drove with me an hour away to go fishing with my father and me for salmon. He caught a beautiful fifteen-pound salmon that day, and we photographed it near my mother's rhododendrons before taking it back to Port Townsend for our supper. My mother led Stanley around her flower garden and they developed an instant rapport—she reciting the names of plants and he often recognizing something aloud before she could tell him, thereby presenting, as unobtrusively as possible, his own credentials as an accomplished gardener.

At some point they got into a lively, but friendly argument about which was the oldest known tree in the world. My mother insisted it was the Bristlecone Pine. Stanley argued that it was the *Metasequoia glyptostroboides,* commonly known as the Dawn Redwood. *"Pinus aristata,"* my mother declared, and stood firm. Over the next several years I passed clippings from various newspapers and gardening journals proving one or the other case back and forth between them. Clearly neither was going to lose this debate. My mother had proudly displayed her own Bristlecone Pine to Stanley before he left, and this caused Stanley to say to me at the end of one of our visits in the East, "I'd like to give your mother a Dawn Redwood. Sometime I will."

The time must have seemed appropriate to him after my father's death in 1982. The idea of the tree had accumulated sufficient significance. I followed instructions and went to the nursery to make the purchase for Stanley. The next day, to my mother's delight and surprise, a truck arrived with the Dawn Redwood. It was planted a little distance from its adversary, the Bristlecone Pine. This seems to have settled the contest between them, and in its place are my mother's ministrations toward the tree itself, referred to now simply as "Stanley's tree."

I tell this story to commemorate the longevity of the man himself as we celebrate his poetry, criticism, and his many personal gifts to the entire literary community in his eightieth year, and to bring us back to kindness, without which the work we do would be bereft of its deepest rewards. Stanley Kunitz's gifts to the literary community and to me personally amount to a debt that can only be answered with thanks and with love, which isn't an answer—but more like two trees, each reputed to be the oldest living tree in the world, growing silently upward, side by side.

UNDER DISCUSSION
Donald Hall, General Editor

Volumes in the Under Discussion series collect reviews and essays about individual poets. The series is concerned with contemporary American and English poets about whom the consensus has not yet been formed and the final vote has not been taken. Titles in the series include:

Elizabeth Bishop and Her Art
  edited by Lloyd Schwartz and Sybil P. Estess
Richard Wilbur's Creation
  edited and with an Introduction by Wendy Salinger
Reading Adrienne Rich
  edited by Jane Roberta Cooper
On the Poetry of Allen Ginsberg
  edited by Lewis Hyde
Robert Bly: When Sleepers Awake
  edited by Joyce Peseroff
Robert Creeley's Life and Work
  edited by John Wilson
On the Poetry of Galway Kinnell
  edited by Howard Nelson
On Louis Simpson
  edited by Hank Lazer
Anne Sexton
  edited by Steven E. Colburn

Forthcoming volumes will examine the work of Langston Hughes, Philip Levine, Muriel Rukeyser, H.D., James Wright, Frank O'Hara, and Denise Levertov, among others.

Please write for further information on available editions and current prices.

Ann Arbor   **The University of Michigan Press**